The Story of
Brunswick Town
&
Fort Anderson

By Franda D. Pedlow
with additional material by
Jack E. Fryar, Jr.

Books
A JEF Publications Company

Previous edition in 1996
This revised edition 2005

Published in the United States of America by Dram Tree Books

ISBN 0-9723240-6-2

Dram Tree Books
2801 Lyndon Avenue
Wilmington, N.C. 28405
(910) 538-4076
dramtreebooks@ec.rr.com

*Discounts available
for bulk buyers.
Call or e-mail for terms.*

Acknowledgements

Many thanks to The Friends of Brunswick Town, represented by Frances Allen, President; and Susie Carson, teacher and friend who was the first to encourage me in this endeavor; and to Jim Bartley, Site Manager of Historic Brunswick Town. These people are responsible for my interest in writing this book. Certainly the staff at the site provided much help. The discovery that I had an ancestor involved with Brunswick gave an additional impetus to my enthusiasm for this very important and little known period of North Carolina history. Special thanks go to my husband Phil for his assistance and support in every phase of this venture.

- Franda D. Pedlow

The love of history introduces you to a wide variety of people. Some of them are brilliant, some of them are eccentric, and some of them...well, let's face it, some of them seem a little nutty compared to the population as a whole. You have to be a little loopy to live your life literally in the past – at least at first glance. After all, camping on a long-dead battlefield in a Cape Fear, N.C. January or February so cold that your lips won't move (all for authenticity's sake) has to be about a half bubble off of plumb! But a closer look reveals that these seeming lunatics understand something that escapes many people. They know that who we were as a people has a great deal to do with who we are, and who we will become. They know the value of passing on to future generations the stories of those who came before, and the simple duty of honoring their sacrifices, which helped make us who we are. So I am fortunate that my love of history has introduced me to some people who are what my mother would call "just good folks." Among them are Jimmy Bartley, Brenda Marshburn, Millie Hart, Chris Jackson, Kent Snyder and everyone else who works to make sure the treasures of Brunswick Town / Fort Anderson will be there for those of us seeking our history now, as well as for those who come seeking it after us.

- Jack E. Fryar, Jr.

Introduction

*I*t might seem improbable that this quiet place on the bluffs of the Cape Fear River could ever have held a place of importance in the shaping of this country. However, there are several reasons for Brunswick Town to be remembered.

It was one of the best ports along the eastern seaboard during the colonial period, so it was a trade center. Exports of tar, turpentine, pitch and lumber provided the majority of Great Britain's naval stores for many years.

Of the five Royal Governors of North Carolina, one was largely responsible for the development of the lower Cape Fear River lands, and another was sworn into office at Brunswick Town in 1734; two lived there from 1754 to 1771; and the last fled from the rebelling state aboard a British warship during the Revolutionary War.

The town was attacked and occupied for several days in 1748 by Spanish privateers during the War of Jenkins' Ear between Great Britain and Spain, before being retaken by a courageous group of Brunswick men and militia from Wilmington. Brunswick Town became the scene of resistance to the Stamp Tax Act of 1765. In what may have been the first open, armed act of rebellion against British rule in the American colonies, Cape Fear men defied English lawmakers and their representatives in the colony a full eight years before the Boston Tea Party.

Brunswick Town was the first county seat of New Hanover County with the Court of Sessions established there in 1729. It was home to great planters, an Associate Justice of the United States Supreme Court, and a plethora of men who pledged their all to win freedom in the Revolutionary War. A century later, it would host another group of native sons who also fought for what they perceived as freedom, this time in a losing cause.

This is the story of Brunswick Town / Fort Anderson.

Contents

Facts About Brunswick

1 - Existed from 1726-1776. Named in honor of King George I of England, who was of the House of Brunswick.

2 - Was the home of two of North Carolina's five Royal Governors: Arthur Dobbs and William Tryon.

3 - Established by Maurice Moore, a wealthy soldier and plantation owner.

4 - In 1729, was made a Township by Assembly Act, with power to erect a church, a courthouse, and a jail.

5 - First town in the Cape Fear region of North Carolina.

6 - Port was the most important one in the colony.

7 - Brunswick was attacked by Spanish privateers in 1748.

8 - Lost power to Wilmington by the 1740's.

9 - Hurricanes and storms destroyed parts of the town.

10- Port supplied a large percentage of the naval stores so vital to keep Great Britain's powerful navy afloat.

11- Became county seat when Brunswick County was established in 1764.

12- Locals successfully defied royal authority by refusing the Stamp Act Tax in 1765. It was one of the first examples of armed citizens standing up against the King's representative with no actual violence occurring.

13- Sacked and some houses burned by the British under Capt. John Abraham Collett in 1776. Town was mostly deserted by then.

14- Fort Anderson built as part of the Cape Fear River defenses constructed by Confederate forces during the Civil War. The earthen fort is built on top of Brunswick's ruins.

15- Fort Anderson falls to Union forces in February 1865, opening the way for the capture of Wilmington. Confederates evacuated the fort following a combined assault by Union naval and ground forces.

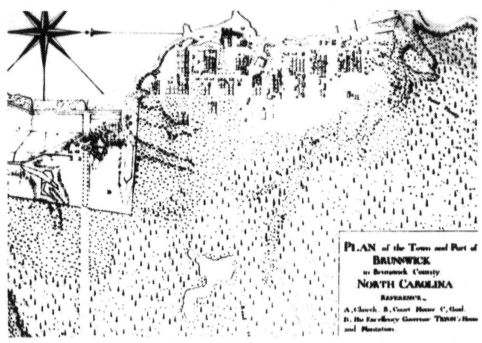

Brunwick was the first settlement on the Cape Fear River to survive beyond two years, and became North Carolina's first and only port with direct access to the ocean.

Beginnings of Brunswick Town

*I*n the early 1700s the settlers in eastern North Carolina were in danger of complete annihilation at the hands of King Hancock's Tuscarora Indians. A desperate call for help brought men from the colonial capitol in Charleston, South Carolina. Two sons of the governor, Colonel James Moore and Captain Maurice Moore, led a relief expedition that finally defeated the Indians.

A year later, on his way back to South Carolina to help put down a serious Indian attack there, Maurice Moore crossed the Cape Fear River at the site of present day Brunswick Town. He thought it was a beautiful spot. The land was high enough to discourage diseases, and was covered with lush forests and game. The river was wide and deep in this section, an easy place for large ships to dock, showing good potential to be a major port.

Moore was the grandson of Sir John Yeamans, who had led English settlers from Barbados to settle at Port Royal in the 1660's. Yeamans' colony overshadowed an earlier group under John Vassals, who had settled on the Cape Fear River in 1664. Vassals' colony set up at the mouth of Town Creek, four miles north of the place where Moore would establish Brunswick Town. The colony lasted for two years, but failed because of a lack of supplies, an

The tomb of "King" Roger Moore at Orton.

inability to get land grants from the Lords Proprietors, and hostile Indians. When Vassals' colony broke up two years later, many of the settlers joined Yeamans' group around Port Royal, to help form what would become Charleston, S.C.

It was 1725 before Moore was able to obtain from the Lords Proprietors the 1500 acres he desired. One of his first moves was to establish Brunswick, which he expected to be a successful business venture. He and his brother, Roger, contributed 340 acres upon which to build the town on the west bank of the river. Another brother, Nathaniel Moore, joined them there.

Maurice drew up a plan for 336 half-acre lots measuring 82.5 x 264 feet, with a common area for a courthouse, church, a graveyard, jail, and other public buildings. There were several streets, with the main one running parallel to the river. The first lots were sold to Cornelius Harnett, Sr. in 1726.

New Hanover Precinct was established in 1729, with Brunswick the seat of government. At the time, North Carolina and South Carolina both laid claim to what was called the "Brunswick Settlements". Soon the dispute was settled, with North Carolina in control of the area south from the

Col. Maurice Moore (left)

Cape Fear to the Little River section. Until 1764, Brunswick was part of New Hanover County.

Brunswick was made the official Port of Entry for all shipping in the lower Cape Fear area in 1731. All ships had to check in and register the cargoes they carried into or out of the river. Being one of the three major ports in North Carolina, Brunswick accounted for a large percentage of the colony's trade.

By then several houses had been built at Brunswick. One of the quotations surviving from the period does not paint a bright picture of the town. Hugh Meredith, writing in 1731, described the town as being "...but a poor, hungry improvided place, consisting of not above 10 or 12 scattering mean houses, hardly worth the name of a village," but he felt "the platform is good and convenient, and the ground high considering the country."

Maurice Moore's brother, Roger, built a plantation adjoining the town and named it Orton. Of the more than sixty plantations that lined the Cape Fear River up until the end of the Civil War, Orton is the only one surviving today. Orton was burned by local Indians as soon as it was completed. Enraged, Roger Moore gathered a force of men and set about destroying the Indians. In a final battle across the river at Sugar Loaf, Moore smashed the natives, nearly exterminating them. Survivors moved inland and joined tribes away from the coast. Moore rebuilt Orton a few years later. Roger became known as "King Roger" because of his bearing and demeanor. The title is even on his crypt in Orton's colonial cemetery.

Roger Moore built his Orton Plantation on a high bluff overlooking the Cape Fear River.

British officer-turned-pirate Stede Bonnet hangs in Charleston after being captured on the Cape Fear.

Pirates

From the time of exploration, pirates roamed the southeastern coast and certainly caused much anxiety for the colonists. In those days the loss of a ship filled with supplies could devastate an entire town, and the capture of passengers was worse.

Rumors that North Carolina Governor Charles Eden was helping Edward Teach, the notorious pirate more commonly known as Blackbeard, reached the Moores in 1718. Maurice and his brother-in-law, Edward Moseley, felt that there was no way to prove this except to enter the Governor's office and search his papers. Never lacking in self-confidence, they did just that. Nothing incriminating was found, and Eden fined both men for their actions. But Blackbeard remained a threat. The Moores joined with other coastal planters and merchants in asking for help from North Carolina's sister colony, Virginia. Governor Spottswood dispatched a British sloop from the James River to capture or kill the pirate. Under the command of Lieutenant Robert Maynard, the sloop caught up with Blackbeard in Ocracoke Inlet. The fight was vicious, but the pirate was killed.

During that same year Stede Bonnet, called by some the Gentleman Pirate, was active along the Carolina coast. Bonnet had been a major in the British army who came to Barbados to manage a sugar plantation. According to Daniel Dafoe, Bonnet took to piracy to escape a nagging wife. With two

Not all pirates who cruised the Cape Fear were men. Anne Bonney and Mary Read were two pirates of the fairer sex who prowled for loot along the North Carolina coast.

captured vessels, Bonnet sailed his ship, the *Revenge*, into the Cape Fear River to make repairs. He nestled his ship into the mouth of a small creek near modern Southport, where the vessel could be careened (tilted up on one side) and repairs made to her hull.

Somehow, the news of his location reached Charleston. The governor dispatched Colonel William Rhett in two sloops-of-war to capture the pirate and his crew. Bonnet saw the British ships enter through Old Inlet and quickly put the *Revenge* back out into the river. In a running gunfight that hugged the eastern side of the river channel, all three ships ran aground on the ebbing tide. For hours they slammed shells into each other until the tide began to flow into the Cape Fear again. Rhett's ship was the first to regain water under her keel, and he pulled around to deliver what would have been a devastating broadside into the *Revenge*, still hull-up on the shoals off Bald Head Island. Bonnet saw what was coming and hastily hoisted a white flag. Bonnet and his crew were taken to Charleston and hanged.

Other pirates frequented the Cape Fear and Carolina coast, including Captain Kidd, and Anne Bonney and Mary Read, two notorious women pirates. Thirty years later, in 1748, Spanish privateers (what some people call a kind of legal pirate) raided Brunswick Town during the War of

Jenkins' Ear. But after Blackbeard and Bonnet were dealt with in 1718, the worst of the piracy was over for the Cape Fear area.

Edward Teach, aka Blackbeard, also preyed on shipping belonging to Cape Fear planters. Blackbeard was killed at Ocracoke after Cape Fear planters enlisted the aid of Virginia's governor in the pirate's capture.

Until the construction of the twin bridges over the Cape Fear in the early twentieth century, ferries were the only means of crossing the river from New Hanover and Brunswick Counties.

The Brunswick Ferries

The King's Highway was the only road connecting the northern and southern colonies. The last section of it was completed in 1732, and it lay between the Neuse and the Cape Fear Rivers. Despite the term highway, the road was actually very poor for many of its miles. In the Brunswick area the roads were often impassable. Because of this, most travel along the North Carolina coast in the early years was by water.

A ferry across the Cape Fear was a necessity. Cornelius Harnett bought property from Maurice Moore in December 1726 and began operation of a ferry from Brunswick to a landing on the east side of the river at Sugar Loaf, appropriately named the Haulover. Early ferries were usually rafts, difficult to handle in the swift moving currents of the Cape Fear. The toll for a man with his horse was five shillings, while a person crossing without a horse paid 3 shillings in the 1730s.

Cornelius Harnett owned a tavern near the ferry landing. He shrewdly guessed that food and lodging would be important for weary travelers. One such traveler, saddle sore from bad roads, bored of the unchanging countryside, raw from traveling in bad weather, and lonely for human company, wrote that the taverns – or ordinaries, as they were sometimes called – were inviting establishments.

Next to operate the ferry was a former mariner named Edward Scott, who carried travelers across the Cape Fear until he resigned in 1738. Colonel Thomas Merrick was then awarded the franchise. Merrick had come to Brunswick from Barbados, and bought a large tract of land from Maurice Moore. He ran the ferry for two years before dying.

Roger Moore was granted permission to run the ferry in 1741, though it is thought that he hired others to handle the day-to-day operations. By 1745 John Maultsby (or Maulsby) was running the ferry. He was experienced at it, having run a ferry on the Schuykill River in Pennsylvania.

Darby Egan had begun operating the ferry and an ordinary by 1760. During Egan's tenure, the legislature enacted several changes in how ferries were to be run. A law was passed requiring ferrymen to have no less than two boats to each ferry, and to provide proper pens to receive cattle that needed to be ferried. There was a devastating hurricane in 1761 that opened a new inlet off the southern tip of New Hanover County, and changed the location of the ferry on the eastern side of the river.

The Colonial Assembly passed a law in 1766 requiring ferrymen charging more than four pence a trip to maintain a tavern for the ease of travelers. They also had to provide good and sufficient boats or other craft in good repair to be well attended while transporting travelers and their property.

The governor ordered the establishment of a full-time postal service in 1764, and the Brunswick Ferry was on the route. The next year it was decided that the ferry house on the east side of the river needed to be manned at all times. Mrs. Egan began staying there herself to make travelers comfortable. In 1769 Egan moved the ferry upriver to Wilmington, where he thought he could make more money serving the east bank town that was rapidly overshadowing Brunswick.

The ferry was in operation until the Revolutionary War, when twenty warships of the British navy occupied the mouth of the Cape Fear River, and redcoats began making frequent forays into Brunswick and the surrounding countryside. By then Brunswick was a ghost of its former self, most of the families having moved upriver to new homes in Wilmington. But while the Brunswick ferry ceased to exist in early 1776, ferries remained the only way for most travelers to get from the New Hanover County side of the Cape Fear to the Brunswick County side until the twin bridges were built at Wilmington in the 1930s.

Rivalry With Wilmington

*I*t was readily apparent to anyone visiting the lower Cape Fear that the Moores and their friends were the most influential and powerful people in the region. In fact, the Moores and their extended friends and family were collectively known far and wide as "The Family". They held most of the important government positions, and many served in the Assembly and the Council.

The Family owned the majority of land patents in the Cape Fear region. Of 105,000 acres given in grants, the Moores, their family and friends held 83,000 acres. Roger and Maurice Moore alone are believed to have accounted for 25,000 acres apiece.

Acting as agent for the Lords Proprietors, Governor George Burrington made these grants, allocating 10,000 acres for himself. But being governor over The Family was no easy task. The power the Moores wielded often put them at odds with the new governor, Gabriel Johnston, who took office in a ceremony held at the Brunswick courthouse in 1734. Johnston and the Moores frequently had different ideas about how the colony should be run. In one notable incident, the governor and Maurice Moore both laid claim to a parcel of fertile land north of Wilmington. Johnston ended up on the losing side of the argument, and from then on he began advocating the newer town over the Moores' Brunswick settlement.

The village sixteen miles upriver from Brunswick has been known by many names since it came into existence in 1733. New Carthage, New Liverpool, New Town, and Newton were all names for Brunswick's main competitor before it was finally christened Wilmington in 1740.

Having the governor as an enemy was a powerful disadvantage to the development of Brunswick. Gov. Johnston described conditions at the town as unhealthy, exaggerating the risks of fever and other sickness at the town the Moores founded in official reports sent back to England. In the minutes of the Executive Council for June 5, 1740, he said, "We allow that the Flats below Brunswick may have two feet more water than the Banks below Wilmington. But to balance this, it is notorious that Brunswick is the most sickly unhealthy place in the whole Colony. In the short time Your Excellency has been in the Government no less than three Collectors of the Customs have died there, and in that Space we cant recollect above three Housekeepers who lived at your Excellency's Arrival who are remaining at present. Some few of them indeed removed by reason (as we suppose) of its Sickliness, but the rest as far as we can Judge have been actually killed by the unwholesome water and the Pernicious Vapors rising from ponds and Marshes with which it is almost Surrounded."

Johnston decreed that quit-rents would be paid in Newton instead of Brunswick as early as 1735. These rents were paid in money instead of being paid in trade or services. Controversies concerning this payment were widespread in the colony, and caused a great deal of unrest. The Moores were known for their strong support of local rights, but this time their desires were surely influenced by their fear of losing control of a large section of the lower Cape Fear.

Governor Johnston continued to undermine the fragile foundation of Brunswick until he scored a major coup by having the courts moved to Wilmington in 1740. This removal of government business from Brunswick was the final undoing of the small town, even though the Port of Brunswick did not fade totally away until the Revolutionary War.

In February 1740 notices were given to repeal any and all acts (specifically the Acts of 1729) which "directs the Courts and Elections of County and the Church, Court-House, and Gaol of the said County of New Hanover and St. James Parish, to be held and built at a place called Brunswick..." The location of the Court of Pleas and Quarter Sessions determined the importance of a colonial town, since it was the center of activity. All legal business took place there. Citizens came to buy land, obtain licenses, consult lawyers, serve as jurors, and to get news.

As imagined, a great storm of protest arose at Johnston's actions. One officially expressed sentiment said, "Because the Town of Brunswick was by one Act of Assembly of this Province passed the ...day of November 1729 made a Township, and by virtue of that Law, a power to erect a church, a Prison and Court House, and to hold the several courts of the Precinct therein. That from the encouragement of this Law, many people did undertake, to build and actually built, several good Houses, and made great improvements in and about said Town some years before the village of Newton was erected..."

North Carolina and South Carolina spent years trying to settle on a dividing line that satisfied both states. It would be interesting to speculate what would have happened to the town of Brunswick if South Carolina had succeeded in extending its borders to the Cape Fear and included it. Would it be a large and thriving city today?

St. Philips Anglican Church at Brunswick is the oldest house of worship in the Cape Fear. It has suffered at the hands of both the British and Union armies in the decades since its construction.

Church and Religion

*T*he most prominent ruin in Brunswick Town is St. Philips Anglican Church. This building was completed in 1768 after years of intermittent construction, and is seventy-six feet long by fifty-three feet wide. The brick walls are three feet thick and twenty-four feet high. Inside aisles formed a cross of brick tiles one foot square, with the rest of the floor being made of wood. Pews sat on the wooden floor, except one that sat elevated above the others. This was reserved for Royal Governor Arthur Dobbs, and its exalted elevation is said to have irritated some of the other members of the congregation.

The Vestry Act of 1729 created a church supported by local taxes. James Murray wrote a letter in 1736 saying, "We have the best minister that I have heard in America to preach and read prayers to us every 2d or 3d Sunday at least, and on a cold day a good fire in ye church to sit by." Reverend John LaPierre is known as the first Anglican minister to work in the lower Cape Fear area by 1728, but it isn't known if he is the minister Murray is referring to.

St. Philips parish was established in 1740 and shared a minister, John Moir, with Wilmington's St. James Church. Neither parish was pleased with the arrangement. Brunswick citizens provided Muir with a small house in 1744, and it was probably Moir who taught school there. It is the only school known to have existed at Brunswick, with education usually provided by the families themselves.

Artist's sketch of the inside of St. Philips.

In 1746 Moir became displeased with Brunswick and left, to be replaced by Christopher Biers. Biers remained in the town until 1750. The church remained pastorless for four years, until John McDowell assumed the reins in 1754. He, too, alternated between churches in Wilmington and Brunswick. North Carolina only had five churches at the time, and only the one in New Bern was in anything resembling good condition.

That was the year construction began on St. Philips Church. Monies for the project initially came from the salvaging of the Spanish raider *La Fortuna*, a ship that had blown up during the fighting between privateers and Brunswick militia in 1748. The legislature ordered that the proceeds of the salvage be used to build churches at Wilmington and Brunswick. Construction was slowed by the heavy tax burden brought on by the French and Indian War. Compounding the problem was the fact that while the church was supposed to be used by everyone in the region, residents were widely scattered in farms that ranged well up the Cape Fear River. Additionally, many of the settlers were dissenters of different faiths from the official church.

John McDowell became the full-time minister at St. Philips and was awarded a small house and a glebe of 300 acres. But McDowell never preached with a roof over his head, as construction stopped when the brick walls reached the tops of the windows.

In 1759 a lottery was authorized to raise money for the completion of the church. Governor Arthur Dobbs wanted the church finished, so he got behind the project and signed the bill, even though he didn't approve of lotteries. A year later, Dobbs notified the people that St. Philips, when completed, would become His Majesty's Church in North Carolina. This meant the King would donate to it a communion plate and table, a pulpit, a Bible, and a Book of Common Prayer for the congregation.

Royal Governor Arthur Dobbs

Construction was rapidly underway again, and the roof, complete with belfry, was up in a few months. It was a short-lived accomplishment, though. A summer storm destroyed the roof and caused a halt to construction for more several years.

In 1762 Rev. McDowell gained an additional income as chaplain for Governor Dobbs' family. McDowell wrote of the house being used as the church while construction on St. Philips proceeded slowly along: "...the chapel is a miserable old house, only 24 x 16, and every shower of rain or blast of wind, blows quite thro' it. If I had continued I intended to have purchased it, and to have fitted it up a decent manner and to have made it comfortable for the performance of divine services both Summer and Winter, till the Church might be finished."

The church was complete enough for seventy-three year-old Governor Dobbs set tongues to wagging when he married fifteen-year-old

Justina Davis there in 1763. Despite the gossip and behind the back laughter, the couple seemed happy together. Dobbs lived with his young wife for another two years until he died in 1765. He was buried inside the still unfinished St. Philips. Dobbs left his entire estate to Justina, who later married Governor Abner Nash.

The new Royal Governor, William Tryon, was interested in the completion of the church and contributed personally by making a large donation to the improvement of the graveyard. He also donated window sashes and English glass for the church. After Rev. McDowell died, John Barnett took over the Brunswick flock and lived in Tryon's house at Russellborough, where he was quite comfortable.

In 1768 St. Philips Church was finally finished and dedicated. It was a large and lovely edifice for any colonial town, and must have been very impressive. Archaeologist Stanley South thinks the roof was hipped and the brickwork of Flemish bond with glazed headers.

After Barnett left due to illness, a Reverend Cramp came for two years. The town was without a minister until 1774, when Nicholas Christian served for a year. Christian traveled a great deal to baptize and preach, but found discouragingly small numbers of people to preach to. Many people preferred the less formal services of other denominations.

In 1776 the town was almost deserted when British troops under Captain John Abraham Collett arrived. The redcoats sacked what was left of the town, including the church. The walls were all that remained, and were still there when Confederate troops began construction of Fort Anderson on top of the town ruins in 1862. Despite being shelled by Union gunboats during the fight for the fort in 1865, the walls still stand.

A few of the St. Philips gravestones can still be read, but most of the graves are unknown. There were twelve burials near the altar inside the church, and one more discovered by Dr. Stanley South at the rear of the building.

Artist Art Newton's idea of what St. Philips would have looked like when finished.

Flora MacDonald and her husband were among the many Scotch immigrants who entered America at Brunswick.

Immigrants and Settlers

The first settlers to the Cape Fear were Puritans from New England, who had the idea that they would colonize the river and raise cattle. They must have arrived during the summer months, because the would-be settler stayed only long enough to let loose the livestock they brought with them, fill their water casks, and head back out to sea over the bar at Old Inlet. Other than their cows, the only thing they left behind was a warning to those who came after them to turn around while they could. The mosquitoes must have been particularly bad that summer.

Next came John Vassal's colony at the mouth of Town Creek. Vassals and company came from Barbados and began their new life on the Cape Fear River in 1664. The colony lasted for two years before trouble with the local Indians, and neglect from the Lords Proprietors and Governor Sir John Yeamans in favor of his own colony at Port Royal, all conspired to see the settlers give up on the place the Indians had named Chicora. The region remained unsettled until fifty years later, when the Moore family rediscovered it. Not long after, the Lords Proprietors were relieved of their responsibilities for the colony by the King of England, and it became a royal colony.

Unlike the Lords Proprietors, Royal Governor George Burrington believed the land of the lower Cape Fear should be settled. He saw the potential for commerce and farming, and was willing to grant many acres of land to men applying for a land patent to do just that.

Public land or title to such land, granted to someone is a patent.   He offered inducements such as the establishment of a road south from New Bern to the area.

With a few exceptions the first men to obtain these patents were the Moores and their family and friends.   Some came from the Goose Creek area near Charleston, South Carolina.   They were wealthy plantation owners who came with slaves and household furnishings and took large tracts of land along the river.   Actually, some of these folk left South Carolina because of the diseases prevalent there.   What they had heard about the healthy conditions for living and the expectations for making money encouraged them to make the move.   Several families who had followed James and Maurice Moore to New Bern were also included.

When Gabriel Johnston became governor he encouraged many of his fellow Scotsmen to come to this country.   It was said that 312 Highlanders came from the Isle of Skye itself.   Many of them settled farther up the Cape Fear.   One of those from Scotland was Flora MacDonald, the famous activist with royal sentiments.

The best tracts of land along the river and creeks were quickly taken by the wealthy so there were few places for a small farmer to settle.   Most of the less fortunate had to locate on poor soil covered by scrub pine.   This situation discouraged rapid population growth.

Of course, Brunswick attracted merchants and men who offered necessary services to a trading town.   These men, some with their families, came from other colonies as well as from other countries.

When Wilmington became a thriving town some forward thinking men realized the essential need for a town to be continued at the Port of Brunswick.   They prompted the passage of an act by the General Assembly of 1745 that encouraged settlement in Brunswick.

In 1762 some Moravians came into port from Philadelphia on a small ship of about 23 tons.   Six women squeezed into the captain's meager quarters.   The men did the best they could in the hold along with the captain and crew.   It must have been very uncomfortable on top of the cargo of crates and barrels.

All during the rest of the 1700s immigrants came to the port.   Some remained in the area but most continued up the river to inland towns being established.   They came from many places: England, Lisbon, Isle of St. Michael, Ireland, New York, South Carolina, Isle of Jersey, Massachusetts, Pennsylvania, Switzerland, and others.

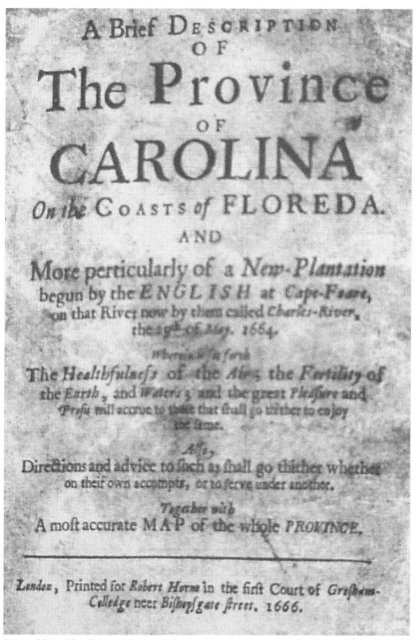

A Brief DESCRIPTION
OF
The Province
OF
CAROLINA
On the COASTS of FLOREDA.
AND
More perticularly of a New-Plantation
begun by the ENGLISH at Cape-Feare,
on that River now by them called Charles-River,
the 29th of May. 1664.

whereunto is set forth
The Healthfulness of the Aire, the Fertility of
the Earth, and Waters; and the great Pleasure and
Profit will accrue to those that shall go thither to enjoy
the same.

Also,
Directions and advice to such as shall go thither whether
on their own accompts, or to serve under another.

Together with
A most accurate MAP of the whole PROVINCE.

_____

London, Printed for Robert Horne in the first Court of Gresham-
Colledge neer Bishopsgate street. 1666.

*Pamphlets like this one touted the many advantages to be had in North
Carolina for those willing to make the voyage to the colony.*

This four pounder cannon was salvaged by archaeologists from the river off of Brunswick in the 1980's. It is believed to have been aboard the Spanish privateer **La Fortuna.** *It is now on display in the Brunswick Visitors Center.*

Spanish Attack

England spent many years intermittently at war with Spain and France. In 1744 the French were fighting British colonists in New England for the third time. That year Governor Johnston, certainly aware that the Cape Fear was a logical place for attack, met with his Council in emergency session to plan for the defense of the area. Johnston called for a defensive site to be found. The Council met at Brunswick soon afterward and decided upon the best locations to search for stable land formations. It was nine months before this was accomplished and voted upon by the General Assembly. A fort was to be constructed on the west side of the river near its mouth. Today this is in the town of Southport. Fort Johnston, named for the governor, was still under construction when an assault actually came.

The nightmare of being attacked by a foreign nation became a reality in September, 1748. Stealthily, two Spanish warships and a captured South Carolina vessel dropped anchor off the bar. At dawn the pilots went out to lead them into the river. By the time the ships were recognized as Spanish it was too late to sound an alarm.

Spaniards were put ashore to capture the slaves working at the fort and nearby plantations. However, it was Sunday and most slaves were at Brunswick.

The townspeople were terrified when they saw the Spanish ships sailing into their port. They quickly grabbed what they could from their homes and fled into the woods. The town was unguarded.

Meanwhile, messengers were sent to neighboring homes and villages asking for help. Commissioner William Dry III mustered men from the surrounding area to attack the Spaniards. This group of about sixty-seven men was armed with pistols, muskets, powder and shot, powder flasks, gunflints, and other supplies to keep them for several days.

Other provisions were gathered. William Moore provided a few hundred pounds of beef and a small cannon, which would be of great value for firing on the ships. William Dry also provided beef and other food, plus three gallons of rum. George Ronalds, a merchant, loaned a Negro slave.

It was three days after the landing that Dry, aided by William Moore (son of Roger), Schenck Moore (son of Nathaniel), Edward Wingate, Cornelius Harnett, Jr., and William Lord, led the counter-attack that completely surprised the Spaniards. Along with militia reinforcements from Wilmington, the Brunswick men filtered back into the town. Intent upon transferring loot to their ships, the sailors were unprepared for the attack, and many were killed or captured.

Barrels and boxes of goods, furniture and bedding were strewn between the Spanish ship and the town. Militiamen wheeled their small cannon into position on the high bluff overlooking the wharf and began shelling the enemy ships. The stress of combat must have been too much for the little artillery piece, for suddenly there was a loud explosion. When the smoke settled the cannon had blown apart.

During this time the Spanish sloop fired its cannons at the town, inflicting serious damage. To the great amazement and relief of the Americans, a huge blast ripped the air, and the Spanish flagship seemed to leap from the water. The explosion killed most of the privateers on board. When the ship settled to the bottom, its masts and upper works poked out of the water to mark its grave.

The explosion alerted the second Spanish ship, which had traveled farther upriver. It returned to open fire on the town. The fight went on into the night with neither side able to best the other. The next day the Spaniards decided to cut their loses and sailed away.

William Dry organized men to bury the dead and hired sailors to help bring up anything worth saving from the sunken ship. These men were paid in rum and sugar. Guns, anchors and sails were rescued along with some of the items stolen from the town, such as shoe buckles and jewelry. It has long been thought that a painting of Christ was salvaged from the wreck. It was most likely found in the captain's quarters that must have remained above water. This painting, "Ecce Homo," was given to St. James Church in Wilmington by the North Carolina Assembly, and hangs there now.

The money realized from the sale of the captured Spanish slaves and the goods retrieved from the ship were earmarked by the Assembly to build St. Philips Church in Brunswick, and St. James Church in Wilmington.

This attack certainly remained in the minds of the townspeople. Their vulnerability was exposed and probably hindered the growth of the town.

The painting **Ecce Homo** *(Behold the Man, in Latin) still hangs in Saint James Episcopal Church in Wilmington.*

Naval stores produced from pine trees at tar kilns like this one were big business for settlers living at Brunswick and elsewhere in southeastern North Carolina.

Exports

The Port of Brunswick certainly lived up to the expectations of the Moores and other people who moved to Brunswick. Docks were built and goods were soon arriving from ships and from the countryside. By 1731 a definite trade existed with several merchants in town and rice growers at nearby plantations.

In the 1700s Great Britain was a nation that depended upon its large navy for its success. It is amazing that the majority of the naval stores used by Great Britain for over 30 years were shipped from the Port of Brunswick. In 1705 the English parliament had approved a bounty to be paid to anyone shipping these items, so production was further encouraged and more lucrative.

A geography professor might point out that without the pine tree much of North Carolina would have washed away. It should also be realized that the products from pine trees brought a great amount of money and importance to Brunswick. North Carolina was indeed blessed with pine trees from the coastal plains to the sand hills. Tar, pitch, and turpentine were extracted from these trees and exported.

The main use of tar was to preserve rope; turpentine was an important ingredient of paint; and pitch was essential for the caulking of ships. Lawrence Lee described the time-consuming process of resin extraction in his book *History of Brunswick County*. Crude or common turpentine was the resin as it flowed from the living tree. The tree was "boxed" or incised in the winter; then the warm sun of spring and summer drew out the crude turpentine. Distilled or oil of turpentine was obtained. Tar was resin forced from pine wood by burning in a kiln—a saucer-like excavation in the ground, surface covered with clay and an underground wooden pipe declining outward from a hole in the center of the clay circle to a pit a short distance away. Pine, cut into small strips, was stacked on the floor of the kiln, covered with turf, and ignited. Burning was controlled by regulating the amount of air permitted through holes punched in the turf cover, and by the placement of the holes themselves. Juices, tar, flowed down the floor and through the pipe into a barrel in the pit. Pitch was made by boiling the tar in open pits or in iron cauldrons. It was constantly stirred until thick, then removed to barrels. Three barrels of tar yielded about two barrels of pitch. Without large parcels of land and the use of slaves to do the difficult work it is unlikely the business would have been profitable.

The forests yielded other products for export. Lumber from hardwood trees as well as pine was cut by hand or at a mill. Masts for ships, barrel staves, shingles, planks and lumber for building were cut for use locally or for export. Lumber products were responsible for seventy-five per cent of all exports from North Carolina in 1774.

For several years immediately before the Revolutionary War the Port of Brunswick shipped more naval stores to Great Britain than any other port in the world. Shipments from all of the colonies in 1772 totaled 185,951 barrels (144,932 of tar; 20,381 of pitch; 20538 of turpentine). Shipments from Brunswick Town totaled 59,006 barrels (49,207 of tar; 4,575 of pitch, 5,224 of turpentine). This was more than the combined totals of the other four North Carolina ports, and was 32% of the totals shipped by the combined other colonies.

Other exports consisted of rice, indigo, corn, furs deerskins, and tobacco. Records show that though the rice and indigo exports were relatively small, they comprised almost the total shipping of these items from the rest of the province. Harry Merrens included the chartat the top of the next page in his book *Colonial North Carolina in the Eighteenth Century*. Ships left Brunswick Town bound for other ports in the colonies, the West Indies, London, Bristol, Ireland and Europe.

Exported from Brunswick:	1768	1769	1770	1771	1772	1775
Barrels of rice	84	73	487	620	52	418
Pounds of indigo	646	264	254	222	1304	1686

Tar, pitch and turpentine were all made from the sap of longleaf pines, plentiful trees around Brunswick in the colonial period. Slaves here tap a tree to get the sap. North Carolina was the largest producer of naval stores in the world when Brunswick was in its prime.

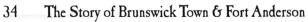

Sloop

Snow

Shipping and Imports

*A*ccording to records the size of ships sailing into the Cape Fear River ranged between 300 tons to less than 50 tons gross weight. The smaller ones could trade at most ports along the eastern seaboard. These lighter vessels, such as the two-masted schooner or the single-masted sloop (both of which were rigged fore and aft), were most often seen in port. Since they weighed less than 50 tons they were able to sail farther up the river.

The ship carrying the majority of naval stores was a brig, or brigantine. It was two-masted and weighed about 100 tons. The largest vessel seen tying up at Brunswick and drawing a crowd to the docks would be the square-rigged ship with three masts and a bowsprit; and the snow, also square-rigged, with its masts placed differently. Averaging 150 tons these transatlantic ships were limited in their ports of call. The latter two were more popular for passengers due to their size and relative comfort. Most cargo ships had accommodations for a few passengers.

Up the river about twenty miles from its mouth lay a shallow area known as The Flats. This was located five miles beyond Brunswick. Silt from Town Creek caused the river to be only ten feet deep at this spot. Ships requiring a deeper draft could go no farther. It was because of the Flats that Brunswick was designated as the official port for the area in 1729.

Brunswick was a highly successful port, and the future looked bright for Maurice Moore's investment. In 1731 forty-two ships were recorded trading there. Ninety ships registered in 1763, and one hundred forty-seven in 1772. In its heyday, 1773-1776, the port saw over three hundred ships carrying cargoes in and out.

There was some ship building in the lower Cape Fear area and at least one ship was constructed at Brunswick. Because it was an established port, it was natural that several ship owners lived there. Thomas Mulford, Capt. Magill and Richard Quince conducted a steady trade with their ships. Other area ships were the brig *Orton*, the *Wilmington* and the schooner *Rake's Delight*.

Thomas Mulford was owner and master of a schooner named the Brunswick Packet that traded mainly with colonial ports to the north. He owned a large house called Prospect Hall on log 337 at the north end of town that he left to his daughters. There were lovely Delft tiles found in the ruins of this house that had decorated the fireplace.

From the earliest days of settlement pilots were needed to guide vessels through the constantly changing and dangerous shoals, and over the main bar near Southport. These men lived nearby, and when a ship was spotted they would row out to meet it and guide it into port. There was no regulation over this profession until 1751. Further rules passed in 1764 limited the number of pilots to twelve, and designated eight of these to work from the bar at Brunswick. The rest piloted from the town to the Flats or to Wilmington.

Imports included the numerous staple goods needed by all of the people as well as quality items brought in for the plantation owners, the Royal Governors, and wealthy townspeople. Among the many imports were tea, powder, shot, guns, lead, iron, rope, sail cloth, linen, silks, cloth and stockings, rugs, furniture, glass, dishes, candles, leather saddles, shoes, toys, horses, and hay for animal feed.

One ship from the West Indies brought in two negroes, fifty hogsheads of rum, one thousand bags of salt, coffee and molasses. From Jamaica came tobacco.

Money from taxes on these imports was used to purchase buoys and beacons needed to mark the Cape Fear River shipping lanes.

In the New Hanover Safety Committee Minutes there are some interesting notations concerning a few ships. On December 20, 1774, a 45-ton schooner, *Bobbin Joan*, owned by Richard Quince of Brunswick was listed with a cargo from the West Indies of molasses. On December 26,

1774 the 45-ton sloop *Hibernia*, owned and captained by James Donovan and registered in Brunswick, arrived from the West Indies with a cargo of salt, sugar, and molasses. On March 20, 1775 the *Clementine* was lost on the bar of the river. Its cargo of paper for newspaper was rescued and put ashore the same day in Brunswick Town. The *Ranger*, registered in Brunswick to owner and Captain Magill, was allowed to carry deerskins to New York on October 16, 1775 in spite of the restrictions on trade by the colonial government.

Due to the fear of diseases arriving on ships, by 1751 all arriving vessels were examined by the commander of Fort Johnston. The ship's captain was required to report under oath of any sickness on board. By 1764 a law was passed requiring the cargo holds of ships to be washed with vinegar and smoked with brimstone.

Brig

Residents of the Cape Fear and coastal North Carolina traveled by water most of the time, due to a lack of good roads.

Traveling

From William Logan's Journal

"...waited half an hour for the boat to come over, but in vain, we returned to Wilmington & after dinner sett out for the Lower Ferry in hopes the Wind would fall & we might get over in the evening to Brunswick, but we were disappointed, for instead of falling it increased much, & by night blew almost a Hurricane at So. West & after raining hard, then shifted immediately to N. West, & blew full as hard all night & cleared up. One Jno. Malsby keeps this Ferry; he lived formerly at the Middle Ferry on Skuykill, but left it and came to the Wilderness Country in hopes of getting an Estate, by the purchase of Lands, but is much mistaken or I am. We were kindly entertained here but as the House is new, & no glass to be had for their Windows, & many are holes & the Wind very high at N. West, I slept miserably, the air coming on me almost from head to foot, but thro' Mercy go no Col, tho' I was very apprehensive of it.

Fifteenth Day – Here we were detained by the Wind continuing to blow so hard that we could not cross the Ferry, which is full three miles wide, till two o'clock, so that we staid here to dine, which we did on a piece of Boiled beef & a good Roast Turkey, and...after dinner went over to

Brunswick (or Old Town) mentioned before, and put at Blenheim's. Here we met with a Snow bound for London with Pitch & Tar and wrote to Elias Bland & John Hunt by her & afterwards went to sup with Jno. Wright, who had before invited us to drink Tea & afterwards to this Supper, which was very handsome for their circumstances, which I imagine are but low.

He was so kind as to get a fowl roasted for us to take with us to eat on the road as he said we should meet with no publick House, which we accepted of.

8th, Sixteenth Day. Arose this morning by break of day having lodged but indifferently & after breakfasting on Tea Set out for Lockwood's Folly abt. 1/4 before seven...I would just observe that all that part of North Carolina that we came through is a poor flat Sandy soil & scarce any thing grown on it but Pines & a coarse Grass in many places, on which their Cattle feed, but one meets now & then with what they call Savannah's, very little better than the rest, only that it bears much more Grass & is better Range.

The People, especially those that live most Southerly are very indolent & lazy & keep Negroes to do their work, which they half starve, allowing no more in general than a half a peck of Indian Corn a week & a pint of Slat, & no Cloaths but a Breech Clout.

The Cattle they raise they have no manner of trouble with for so soon as a Cow calves she is turned into the woods to shift for herself & Calf, which they brand & mark & keep no Dairy's nor milk their Cows but when by chance they come home."

The Chronicles of the Cape Fear River 1660-1916, by James Sprunt, includes the following quote.

"1734 visit to Cape Fear...reach Little Charlotta by dinner time...15 miles from the Ash's, or Little River; dined there, in afternoon crossed ferry where intended to sleep. Reached there 8 same after crossing ferry. It (Lockwood's Folly) has not been settled more above 10 years. Left about 8 next AM & by 2 had reached Town of Brunswick which is chief town in Cape Fear; but with no more than 2 of same horses which came w/us from S.C. (14 men) We dined there in afternoon. Mr. Roger Moore hearing we were come, was so kind as to send fresh horses for us to come up to his house & were kindly received by him; he being the chief gentleman in all Cape Fear. His house is built of brick & exceedingly pleasant 2 miles from town & 1/2 mile from R. Eleazar Allen house nearby."

We have this quote from Hugh Finlay, 1774 about the road from Charleston to Wilmington. It was "certainly the most tedious and disagreeable of any on the Continent of N. America." Concerning a causeway and ferry to Wilmington north of Brunswick, he wrote, "The island is a swamp, the road is laid with logs of trees, many of them are decay'd, so that the causeway is quite broken and full of large holes, in many places 'tis with difficulty that one can pass it on foot, with a horse 'tis just impossible." Finlay felt better about the road from the ferry along the west side of the river. He said, "After the two ferrys there's 13 miles of pretty good road, tho' some parts of it are heavy sand, all the way through a miserably poor pine barren."

Alexander Schaw, a Scotsman who visited in the area wrote about the road conditions in 1775.

"From Fort Johnston at the mouth of the river to Brunswick is twelve miles. From Brunswick to Wilmington there are two roads: one goes up the right side of the river upon which Brunswick stands and crosses two ferries opposite to Wilmington, occasioned by the river being there divided by a large swampy island, through which there is very bad road of a mile and a half. The length of this road is reckoned sixteen miles. To go by the other road, one must cross a ferry at Brunswick of a mile over, from whence to Wilmington is about ten miles. Every part of these roads is more or less sandy. Some of them for miles together is very deep, as the surface often is pure white sand, without a particle of soil to bind it together. This is the case with almost every part of the province near the sea.

The road on both sides of the river cross a few water runs, which in the country are called creeks; they are generally swampy along the sides, which are crowded with trees, brushes, vines, and brambles. Over all these creeks are wooden bridges."

Schaw's sister Janet traveled with him that same year and found the ship from the West Indies to be "neat, clean, and commodious".

Travel by ship depended upon the weather and winds. Usually it took four to five days to reach the Cape Fear River from New York; about two weeks from the West Indies; and three to eight weeks from England.

Col. James Moore

Judge Alfred Moore

Col. Maurice Moore

About the People

*B*runswick was well represented in government throughout its existence. It was home to soldiers, ship captains, and men who would play significant parts in the formation of the state and the struggle for independence. Some of the delegates to the Assembly and Congress in the later years were:

1774   Robert Howe: representative from Brunswick Co. in New Bern to help plan for a new government

1775   Howe and John Rowan: delegates to Assembly in New Bern; Howe, Robert Ellis, Parker Quince, Thomas Alton, Roger Moore to Assembly in Hillsborough

1776   Maurice Moore, Cornelius Harnett, Archibald McLean, Lewis Dupree, William Lord: delegates to the State Congress in Halifax which formed the North Carolina Constitution

Among others, the Safety Committee included: James Bell, William Cains, Thomas Davis, Wm. Lord, Robert Ellis and Richard Quince.

In 1767 Brunswick County had a population of 1095 blacks and 224 white people. There were almost 200 families by 1772 with slaves in less than half. William Dry had 128 slaves in 1769 and Richard Quince had 155 in 1772. No one in the entire state had more slaves.

In 1772 females headed only 17 families. Widows were quick to remarry.

Lack of knowledge and unsanitary conditions contributed to the many early deaths of the colonial period. Those who lived in Brunswick were subject to agues (violent fevers alternating with chills, usually malarial), pleurisies (inflammation causing painful, difficult breathing), and bilious complaints (resulting from ailment of bile or liver). Nearby swamps were breeding grounds for the anopheles mosquito that carries malaria. With ships coming into port from other places, it is certain some of the sailors carried diseases.

There were occasional epidemics. Henry Johnston wrote in October 1770, "A Terrible Fever Has made Sad Havock in this part of the country. Scarce a Family but wears mourning for one or more of Its Branches." In 1777 there was a sickness called a plague that killed two well-known brothers (Judge Maurice Moore and General James Moore, who was home in between battles) the same day.

There were a few days of excitement in town when Governor Tryon sent a young panther to King George III. There is no record of the type of reception the animal received.

It should not be thought that culture was entirely missing. At least once there was a troop of actors in Brunswick. We do not know what plays were presented, but one actor was fine enough to be mentioned by Governor Tryon in a letter to the Bishop of London.

There were dock sales advertised by ship captains when in port with damaged goods, or when an item had been tampered with. The captain was responsible to the shipper so he needed to get some payment for items refused for various reasons by merchants. Cloth was sent in large rolls, and it was not unusual for a sailor to cut off a piece for his own use. When the bolt was measured and found short the merchant did not have to take it. The townspeople could get a bargain at these sales.

Another way to save money was to build your house with the cellar a foot or two below ground level. Since cellars were not taxed, even though essentially the first floor of a house, this was a common practice. These cellars could then be used tax free for businesses such as shops. If there were two floors above the cellar the top floor could be tax free if constructed with formers. This allowed the top floor to be considered an attic.

The majority of the people living in Brunswick were considered middle class with very few of the lower class. Slaves were as numerous as whites. They were allowed to marry, and each family had its own hut and plot of ground for a garden. And, of course, the river helped with a steady supply of food. From the number of fishhooks and lead line-sinkers found at the town it is known that fishing was a popular activity for boys as well as slaves.

The upper class consisted of plantation owners with more than 10 slaves, a few professional men, prominent public officials, some of the more important merchants, and ministers of the Church of England.

In *Tales and Traditions of the Lower Cape Fear 1661-1896,* by James Sprunt, there is a quotation from a Dr. Brickell from Dublin, who visited the Cape Fear region in 1737. He noted that the people he saw were "comfortable and prosperous, hospitable and kindly. Planters cultivated rice, several sorts, some bearded others not so; besides there was the white and the red rice, the latter the better. Indian corn, fruits plentiful; game abundant; cattle thrived and fattened, horse racing, wrestling and foot-racing favorite amusements. Women were well featured, brisk and charming in their conversation and as finely shaped as any in the world. They marry very young, some at thirteen or fourteen. A spinster of twenty is reckoned a stale maid. The houses are filled with healthy children."

It was also reported that "Mr. Harnett entertained his patrons at the Inn with a liberal diet of beef, pork, venison, wild and tame fowl, fish of several delicate sorts, roots (vegetables), several kinds of salads, good bread, butter, milk, cheese, rice, Indian corn, hasty pudding, rum, brandy, cider, persimmon beer, cedar beer, Indian tea, etc."

George Minot, who married into "The Family" and inherited a plantation through his wife, told others that his property was situated in "the best neighborhood". He listed his neighbors as "Mr." or "Esq." or used a military title. He described them as "Persons of fashion and Education and Live in a Genteel manner and most of Em had University Education, Who keep 3 packs of dogs among em for Deer hunting And very often have matches of Horse Racing in the neighborhood, which they very much delight in and are all Living within 3 miles of my House here."

Another visitor, Miss Janet Schaw, wrote of her observations in 1775. "Grapes grow wild and abundant. A large red one bruised and fermented made as good a wine as some imported. Deer plentiful and their meat made delicious soup. The rivers are full of fish. Bears are a problem since they hunted the pigs."

Hurricanes have long been the scourge of people living in southeastern North Carolina, including at Brunswick.

Weather

*T*he climate of Brunswick was certainly mild for most of the year, with snow or ice occurring only occasionally. The heat and humidity that hung heavily in the summer air were dispelled by ocean and river breezes for those who lived near water. Inland, it was hot and miserable for workers and farmers. Many visitors mistakenly took the heat induced lethargy as laziness, and commented as much in letters and journals recounting their visits to the Cape Fear. Under such conditions the locals may have been misjudged.

Northeasters and hurricanes gave the area a great deal of trouble in spite of the distance to the ocean. There was a terrible hurricane in 1761 that lasted for several days. It was so sever that a London magazine wrote about it.

"A storm or hurricane began on Monday September 20, 1761 and continued till Friday following, but raged with most violence on the 23rd. Many homes were thrown down, and all the vessels except one, in the Cape Fear River driven on shore. It forced open a new channel for that river, at a place called haul-over, between the Cedar House and the Bald Head. This new channel was found on sounding to be 18 feet deep at high water, and is near 1/2 mile wide."

The fact that news from Brunswick would be reported in a British publication indicates the importance of the area to them.

Governor Tryon was quite impressed with the storm damage as he wrote in a letter, "The fury of its influence was so violent as to throw down thousands and I believe from reports hundreds of thousands of the most vigorous trees in the country, tearing some up by the roots, others snapping short in the middle. All the Indian corn and rice leveled to the ground and the fences blown down, add to this upward of twenty saw mill dams carried away with many of the timber works of the mills, and lastly scarce a ship in the river that was not drove from her anchor and many received damage." Tryon blamed the hurricane on a comet seen in the skies a short time earlier.

In 1769 another devastating hurricane hit the lower Cape Fear area and this one destroyed the courthouse and some houses in town. Ships sustained damage when blown from their moorings. After this storm the population declined as people sought the safety of Wilmington.

George Demmy built this model of Russellborough, then photographed it as the sun rose over the river, creating a picture of what the real house might have looked like on a misty Cape Fear morning.

Russellborough

*T*his is one of the most historic house sites in North Carolina according to Stanley South, archaeologist, who excavated its ruins in 1965 and 1966.

Captain John Russell of His Majesty's sloop *Scorpion* built a two-storied house between Brunswick and Orton Plantation that he named Russellborough. This is the name that is used today to describe the remains of the mansion.

Governor Arthur Dobbs bought the unfinished house in 1758 and moved there from New Bern, North Carolina. He moved for two reasons. First, he found the cost of renting too high in New Bern. Second, disease was too common there. He expected life in Brunswick to be an improvement. He renamed the house Castle Dobbs.

After Dobbs' death in 1765 William Tryon became governor and bought the property for his home. He named it Castle Tryon. These governors certainly wanted important sounding names for their home. When Governor Tryon left in 1770 for his new "Palace" in New Bern, William Dry III, Collector for the Port of Brunswick bought the property and renamed it Bellfont.

The ruins of Russellborough, just north of Brunswick between the town and Orton.

The British burned the mansion at the beginning of the Revolutionary War along with all its elegant furnishings.

There is an accurate description of the house in a letter written by Gov. Tryon in 1765, soon after he moved into it. He writes, "This house which has so many assistances is of an oblong square, built of wood. It measured on the outside faces forty-five feet by thirty five feet and is divided into two Stories exclusive of the Cellars; the parlour is about five feet above the surface of the Earth. Each Story has four Rooms and three light Closets. The Parlour below and Drawing Room are 20 x 15 feet each: Ceilings low. There is a Piaza runs around the House both stories of ten feet wide with a Balustrade of four feet high, which is a great security for my little Girl. There is a good Stable and Coach Houses, and some other Out Houses."

There were peach, apple, fig and other fruit trees plus a formal garden, vegetable and herb gardens on the property.

This letter along with the information from Stanley South's archaeological excavations gives us a very accurate picture of the house. A model was made by George Demmy, archaeologist, who created it by using historical information of the period along with written data and evidence from the digs. To create the exact scene of the setting, the model was placed on the riverbank where the house stood. A photograph was taken as the sun rose to give us this realistic view from the 1700s.

In the basement Stanley South found the floors were made of Dutch brick and the area divided into several rooms. He discovered remains of a flintlock musket, hinges, and a large lock for a door with the brass key in place. Pieces of a large jar were found and painstakingly put together.

Crucibles are containers that are capable of resisting great heat and are used for melting or fusing metals. Quite a few of them were found in one room. They were most likely used by a silversmith; but there is no clue as to why they were there.

The storage area for wines and other liquors was a jumble of broken and melted bottles. Many still had W. Dry's seal, "W Dry Cape Fear 1766" on them. Wealthy men ordered bottles by the crate in those days. These were made with their own seal on the shoulder of each bottle. Rum, wine, and other liquids were shipped in barrels or kegs and were often emptied into bottles upon arrival. There were about 150 of Dry's seals found at the site. Others were found imprinted with "Pyrmont Water". These bottles had held special spring water from Waldeck, Germany.

An especially important find was a tunnel in one corner of the foundation. It led downhill for a short distance toward the river. This is thought to have been a garbage area. However, it was filled with many items that are now in the museum: wine bottles and goblets, plates, bone handled knives, an intact pottery jar, and other excellent articles.

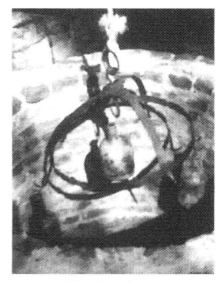

Bottles and a device to keep them cool in a well are among artifacts found at Russellborough.

The tunnel was also used for a sewer. A privy was located on the porch above it and wastes from it were thrown into the opening of the tunnel. Servants would have carried out this task and would have dumped water into the hole to flush it.

Another interesting discovery was a brick-lined well in the basement. Whole bottles were found in and around it, but the surprise was a metal device with hooks. Probably bottles of wine were attached and lowered into the water to be kept cool. It is little wonder that Russellborough was known as a most hospitable home.

South found the place where a wooden cabinet had stood before the fire set by British Captain Collett in 1776. Its location was determined by the appropriate hardware found on the floor. There were straight razor blades, a still full medicine bottle, tea kettle and cups nearby that were probably stored in the cabinet.

Governor Tryon had an outside kitchen built when he moved into his castle in 1765. Supposedly it was 30 feet by 40 feet. About 40 feet from the foundation of the house, Dr. South found a stone foundation that must have

This artist's drawing of what Russellborough may have looked like is from James Sprunt's **Tales and Traditions of the Cape Fear River.**

been the kitchen, because it had the base of an oven connected to a large, seven-foot fireplace.

Excavation showed areas for cooking, servants' rooms, and storage. Outside was a three foot by one foot round pit where South and his staff found an incredible 2,320 fragments of dishes. From these they were able to completely restore forty items. These items consisted of bowls, plates, platters, teacups and saucers, sauce boats, pitchers, jugs, and chamber pot. The pieces were so thickly packed in the pit that no sand had sifted in around them. There were also bottle seals and pieces in the pit that weighed 163 pounds. South figured this to be approximately 108 bottles. This was a large number for an era when bottles were costly and reused.

South told in his notes how these fragments were treated. "In restoring objects from a pit such as this the fragments are first carefully washed, then the catalogue number is written on each piece. They are then separated into piles according to types based on color, hardness, texture, design, etc., and then from these groups individual dish fragments are separated whenever possible. These selected fragments are then glued together. If pieces are missing when all gluing is completed these areas are filled with water putty. The restored sections are then painted to match the original color of the dish, and designs are completed whenever possible. The restored vessel is then ready for exhibit in the Brunswick Town Visitor Center Museum."

Millstones were another discovery in the cellar. These were of limestone that is not from this part of the continent. South discovered that hundreds of limestone millstones were shipped to the colonies from Yucatan, so perhaps that explains their origin.

Delftware chimney tiles suggest that even the fireplace of Russellborough was built with style and artistry in mind.

The Publick House at Brunswick was a center of social activity and commerce.

Publick House

*L*ot 27 at the south end of the town has a stone wall around three sides of the lot, with brick steps in the center front for an entrance. This is a six-room ruin 18 feet by 70 feet. The rooms were side-by-side, 10 feet wide with a fireplace in each. It is much like a modern motel. Publick House is the name assigned to it by Stanley South, archaeologist.

During excavation items were found that would be attributed to sewing or tailoring. Stanley South lists "thousands of brass pins, hundreds of glass beads, large number of copper and bone buttons, brass buckles, twenty-eight sleeve buttons, fourteen thimbles and a number of pairs of scissors". He writes of two sleeve buttons made of 1747 and 1758 Spanish coins and of a small silver spoon that had belonged to Margaret Hill. Three whole hen eggs were found when digging in the yard. South found the habit of throwing broken pottery, bottles and other items into the back yard most helpful in learning about daily life. Some of these dumps were several feet deep in trash.

At this building a compass was found that was intact. A single blade pocketknife had a Malay inscription, "Allah the divider" on one side and "there is no god but God" on the other. Since the British East India Company did most of its business by trading with England, it would be reasonable to have some of those sailors in Brunswick. Oriental china supporting this idea was found in most of South's excavations.

Meals, drinks and more were served to customers of the Publick House, or Ordinary.

Oyster roasts have been popular for centuries, and there was a roasting pit at a corner of the Publick House and at several other houses.

South also found pieces of American Indian pottery dating from the 1760s. He thought this unusual, for it showed their presence in the area much later than was previously known. Supposedly none were left after Roger Moore and his slaves had dispatched the last of the Indians in the late 1720s.

Benjamin Franklin published two letters he received from Hugh Meredith in May of 1731. Parts were concerning Brunswick.

"They have now at Brunswick Quarterly courts of Common Please, and Officers of the Peace, and begin to fall into something like a regular Commonwealth: The Inhabitants are mostly such as were born or have lived in the neighboring Colonies; and This would be soon filled with them and others, were the Country less barren, and but tolerably healthful, (which it is far from), for one great Discouragement to settling this Place is now quite removed, to wit the Indians who drove away or cut off those who attempted the settling it here several times, first the New England Men, then the Barbarians, and last my Countryman Thomas James, who Settlement they plundered and burnt, and murdered him and his Family. But now there is not an Indian to be seen in this place; the Senekas (who have always liv'd in Amity with the English) with their Tributaries the Susquehannah and

Tuskarora Indians having almost totally destroy'd those called Cape Fear Indians, and the small Remains of them abide among the thickest of the South Carolina inhabitants, who daring to appear near the out Settlements, for the very name of a Seneka is terrible to them, as indeed it is to most of these southern Indians: So that I cannot but think both the Carolinas as safe as any of the English Colonies on the Main from any future Indian War."

A brass plate fragment, with most of the name "Brunswick" faint but legible, was an interesting find, as were some coins, and a pipe bowl with designs of Indian arrows, a lance, sword, horn, and fleur-de-lis. Most of these items can be seen in the museum at the Brunswick Town Visitor Center.

Ballast stones from incoming ships were used in building the foundations of most of the houses in town. These stones were ones that had been rounded by glaciers in the Ice Age. They were stored in the holds of the trading ships as needed for buoyancy if the ships were not carrying a full cargo. At the Brunswick docks the stones were dumped on the edge of the river before loading heavy cargoes of naval stores. These stones were very useful since not many were available in the sandy soil nearby.

Oyster shells were crushed to obtain limestone that was a part of the mixture holding the stones together. These foundations are prominent when touring Brunswick.

 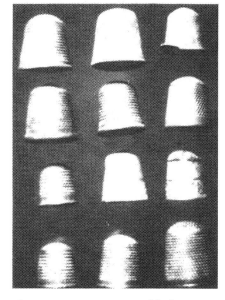

Buttons and thimbles found at the Publick House ruins suggest a person could also get clothing repaired or made there, too.

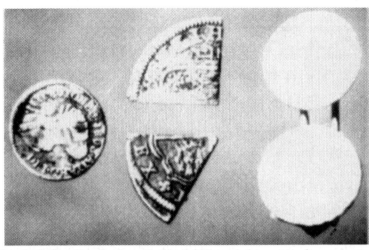

Coins and a clay pipes found where Nathaniel Moore's home stood are among the many treasures uncovered at Brunswick Town by Dr. Stanley South.

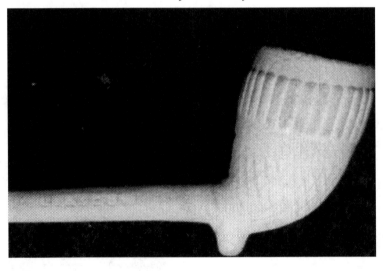

Nathaniel Moore's Front

Nathaniel Moore, younger brother of Maurice, moved to Brunswick soon after it was founded. He built a house on the corner of Front and Cross Street. It is labeled Nath Moore's Front on the trail at Brunswick Town. He sold it to Captain Edmund Scott in 1733. Scott operated the ferry for a time and then had a tavern in his cellar.

When Stanley South excavated these ruins he found that the house had been more carefully built than most. In the ruins was discovered a copper medallion with a man's profile on each side. The words "MARECHAL GERARD - GENERAL LAFAYETTE" were written around the outside edge. This item must have been lost in town after 1830 since Maurice Gerard was Marshall after that year. Also found was a button used by enlisted men between 1814 and 1821, a wig curler, a brass barrel cock, and lead bale clips for use on imported bolts of cloth.

Smokehouse

The smokehouse ruin found on the property of Judge Maurice Moore is the only one of its type known to have been found in any colonial town. The ballast stone foundation measures ten feet square, and a brick firebox was built ten feet away. The two constructs were attached by a ditch, lined with brick, through which the smoke from the firebox could be fanned into the smokehouse to cure the food hung inside. That way, a person did not have to enter the smokehouse to keep the fire burning.

Coins

Surprisingly, many coins were found in the ruins of Judge Maurice Moore's kitchen. He was the son of Brunswick's founder.

This dwelling had a huge nine foot fireplace and an outside round bake oven. Again, broken crockery and knives plus some garbage were swept outside and underneath the floor.

Many of the coins found were too worn to have any markings, but some George II halfpennies were discovered. They were the first coins made for use in the colonies and were made in Ireland in 1732. They have a rose in the middle and a border saying "Rosa Americana". Several were found in Brunswick as were tokens made of sheet metal in England. Companies used them at face value for making change. Some were used in the colonies for trading with the Indians.

The milled Spanish dollar, being real silver, was accepted for trade at Brunswick. The coins would be cut into segments, or "bits", when a lesser amount of money was needed. Two "bits" were found in town that had been cut from a Spanish "piece of eight". This is where the nickname for the quarter originated; two "bits" equaled a quarter or a "piece of eight".

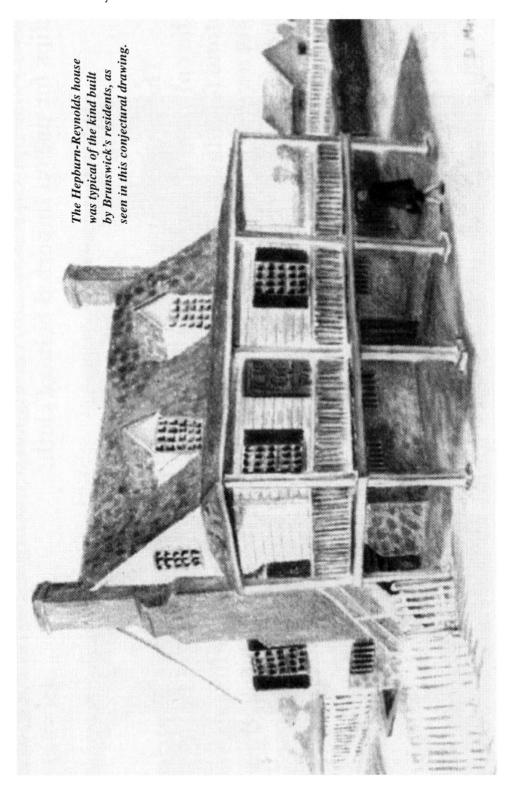

The Hepburn-Reynolds house was typical of the kind built by Brunswick's residents, as seen in this conjectural drawing.

The History of Lot 71

In 1734 two merchants bought Lot 71 from Maurice Moore for the cost of 10 schillings and built a house there. Charles Hepburn had the distinction of refusing to serve as a constable for the Brunswick District and records show that he paid a fine of 10 pounds for punishment. His partner, George Reonalds, was the man who loaned a slave to help in the Spanish attack.

After Hepburn died in 1741, Lot 71 was sold to John Wright for 850 pounds. This was quite a profit but a house was included in the price.

William Lord, Jr., bought Lot 71 in 1748 from John Wright for 900 pounds "lawful money of the province". He died soon after this purchase and his wife Margaret did not or could not pay the taxes. The sheriff took over the property.

In 1759 after remarrying, Margaret managed to buy back the lot from a Moore descendant for 40 pounds.

Another house was built on the lot about 1760 (there are ruins of three dwellings on this property) and Stanley South discovered in his excavations that it had been destroyed about the time of the 1769 hurricane. He surmised that the house was demolished by the storm.

Lot 71 was willed to Dr. John Fergus "Chirurgion" and his wife, Margaret, by her mother, Margaret Lord McCorkall, in 1763. They were living there at the time. Margaret was probably a sister of James Espy, who bought property in Brunswick in 1731. She moved there with him and his family so lived in town for over thirty years. She owned a very popular piece of property.

When the ruins were explored Stanley South found an impressive ruin of a 1730s house measuring 21 feet by 29 feet. There were two basement rooms, with a stone wall between them and separate doors to the outside. There were burned wooden floors still in place, opening onto a brick patio running the length of the house along the back. One of these rooms had served as a storeroom. The second lower room was probably a kitchen. Broken dishes and trash had been thrown outside.

All together with remains of plaster walls found in the trash heap were pieces of imported dishes that included Delft, Wedgewood Creamware, and porcelain from China.

A chimney indicates a two-story house, while stone column footings probably show that the second floor had an overhanging porch. This house extended into the street (which was not too unusual) and it was empty when burned.

When the town is explored, these ruins are clearly marked. It is possible to visualize this house and to understand what it might have been like to live there.

Ballast stones tossed overboard by sailing ships were re-used in home construction.

The Stamp Act Resistance was one of the first open acts of rebellion against British rule.

Stamp Act

C ontroversy over taxes is not a modern phenomenon. The American colonists, with their distance from England and feeling of self-determination, had been somewhat removed from many of the restrictions of British government. To be considered taxable without anyone representing their interest in Parliament was not acceptable to them.

England had just won a war with France and needed money to control new territories. In 1765 a Stamp Act tax was passed by Parliament with encouragement from King George III. Stamps had to be purchased and attached to all legal documents, newspapers, gambling papers, ships' clearance papers, and books or pamphlets. This stamp tax differed from the accepted custom duties levied on trade in that it was a direct personal tax. The British government expected one-third of their new monetary needs for administrating and guarding the new territories to be covered by this tax.

Thus, in the last months of 1765 and the first of 1766, the stage was set for the most important events in Brunswick's history.

When a ship arrived with the stamps on board, angry citizens carrying muskets met the captain at the dock. He did not unload the stamps.

This may have been the first armed resistance in the colonies to the British government.

Gov. Tryon did his best to defuse the anger of the people. He invited a large group of merchants and influential men to dinner in his home, and offered to pay, himself, for stamps on some documents and for wine licenses in certain towns. He received a letter from the men the following day refusing his offer. Tryon may have sympathized with the people but was determined to uphold the law. Citizens of Wilmington protested with such fervor that the stamp master resigned.

In February 1766, two merchant ships, the *Dobbs* and the *Patience*, arrived in the Port of Brunswick. Since they had no stamped clearance papers the ships were not allowed to unload.

William Dry was the Port Collector and held the ships' papers after British Captain Lobb seized the ships. Other ships came into the river in the following days, but some escaped. Barrels of naval stores were soon overflowing the warehouses and were being stacked along the streets. Citizens were upset that all trade had come to a standstill. Court could not be held, newspapers were unavailable, and staple items were needed. Wills could not be proven and there were no marriage licenses issued.

When the North Carolina attorney general ruled that the ships must sail to Nova Scotia for trial, all frustrations erupted.

A group of men who had a common passion for the cause of the colonists formed an association named the Sons of Liberty. They called for a confrontation with the governor and several hundred men, at least 500 of

Armed men from Brunswick and Wilmington lined the river to stop the stamps from being landed

them armed, marched to his home to demand release of the ships. Tryon stood his ground and refused to deal with the men, but did send word to Fort Johnston to spike the guns to make them useless. He feared the incensed crowd would use them to fire upon the British ships.

The next day a mob of several hundred men marched on Russellborough and demanded Tryon turn over Captain Pennington, a stamp act official.. He was supposedly hiding under the governor's bed but went with the men in spite of Tryon's protest. He and Dry and a few other officials and lawyers were influenced to resign their positions, and to sign documents promising that no stamps would be required or sold in the lower Cape Fear region.

William Dry was Port Collector during the Stamp Act rebellion.

The merchant ships were released and the livelihood of the town was saved. A few months later word came from England that the Stamp Act had been repealed. It had caused suffering for the working class and merchants there, as well as for the wealthy shipping families. With that same repeal came news that Parliament retained the right to levy taxes. It would not be very long before they used those rights.

There are several excellent quotations about this Stamp Act rebellion that show its importance.

"It is well worthy of observation that few instances can be produced of such a number of men being together so long, and behaving so well; not the least noise or disturbance nor any person seen disguised with liquor, during the whole time of their stay in Brunswick; neither was there any injury to any person, but the whole affair conducted with decency and spirit, worthy the imitation of all the Sons of Liberty throughout the Continent."

- The Virginia Gazette 1766

The stamp revolt "took place in open daylight, was led by prominent men of community, with arms in hand, who defied His Majesty's governor,

The signature and seal of
Royal Governor William Tryon.

his navy, and his tax collector. It took place ten years before the Declaration of Independence, nine years before the Battle of Lexington, and eight years before the Boston Tea Party."

- A New Geography of North Carolina by Bill Sharpe

"In no other colony was the resistance by force so well organized and executed. Governor Tryon knew each of his opponents in this struggle; not one made any attempt to disguise himself or to conceal his identity in any way. Acting in a forthright manner, without fear, these men succeeded in preventing the operation of the Stamp Act in North Carolina. In so doing, they gave clear evidence of their support of the belief that Parliament had no right to levy such a tax in America."

- North Carolina Gazette, 1766

Col. Hugh Waddell.

Alamance Battleground in 1848, as drawn by Benson J. Lossing for his **Pictorial Field-Book of the Revolution.**

Regulators

O rdinary men, most of whom were farmers in the Piedmont section of the state, were dealing with tax collectors, sheriffs, and other public officials who were overcharging taxes and keeping a good portion of the money themselves. A group of them had organized and were sometimes overly aggressive in their confrontations with the officials.

Two of the leaders of these men, James Hunter and Rednap Howell, after months of asking for assistance, went to Brunswick to present Governor Tryon with a petition. It stated their grievances and requested Tryon to enforce the laws that would alleviate the problem. He took the petition to Assembly for consultation. His answer to the Regulators was that their complaints did not justify their acts of aggression. He told them to cease organized activities and not to harass officers.

But Tryon apparently didn't understand the degree of discontent among the settlers of the inland precincts. Flagrant abuse on the part of officials using their status as King's officers to line their own pockets, and a royal governor who showed no sympathy for their plight, caused rebellious sentiments to continue festering among the inland settlers until violence erupted at Hillsborough.

The confrontation was prompted by an attack by the Regulators on the courts at Hillsborough, when exasperated farmers stormed the town and beat severeal court officials after ransacking and burning the home of Edmund Fanning, Gov. Tryon's representative and the most powerful man in the Piedmont.

Unlike the first time Tryon mobilized the militia to suppress the Regulator movement two years earlier, this time there would be no half measures. Tryon was detrmined to squash this lingering challenge to royal authority, and the Regulators were determined to see fundamental change in the way the government treated them.

The two sides clashed at Alamance Creek near Hillsborough on May 16, 1771. When the smoke cleared, between seventeen and twenty farmers lay dead, as well as nine militiamen. More than 150 men on both sides had been wounded. Governor Tryon issued a proclamation requiring residents to muster at the battlefield and witness the hangings of six Regulator leaders as an object lesson on the fate of those who failed to heed royal authority.

Governor Tryon warned all lawyers and Crown officials to follow the law. Much of the Regulator activity took place while Tryon was still living at Brunswick. He moved to New Bern in the summer of 1770.

Royal Governor William Tryon saw the Regulator movement as a serious challenge to the King's authority in North Carolina. Here he is seen confronting an angry mob of farmers and other settlers from the interior.

Among those who served in Tryon's forces, Brunswick and the Cape Fear were well represented. Robert Howe, Hugh Waddell, John Ashe and Cornelius Harnett all served under the governor's flag.

Sir Henry Clinton

Brunswick's James Moore was one of two officers elected to lead N.C.'s two regiments of Continentals. He orchestrated the Whig response to the Highlander march that led to the battle at Moores Creek.

Also from Brunswick, John Ashe served as an officer of the Continental Line after participating in the burning of Fort Johnston.

Unrest Along the Cape Fear River

It must have seemed inevitable that the problems the colonists experienced with the British government would bring on hostilities. There was much talk of the consequences of refusing to accept the laws and taxes being imposed, which curbed the independence of those in the colonies. Eventually some who felt strongly about these encroachments upon their rights were prepared to fight for them.

In 1773 John Quincy of Boston, an excellent lawyer and zealous protector of home rule, visited Brunswick for five days. He came in order to discuss future Patriot actions, and talked with several of the influential men there about the problems with Britain. William Dry, Robert Howe, Cornelius Harnett, and Richard Quince were in that group. Nothing is known of their conversations, but some people thought that the war was actually planned then and there.

John Quincy called Cornelius Harnett the "Samuel Adams of the south" and said Robert Howe was a "Man of the work, the sword, and the buck".

Howe was an important member of the legislature and a brigadier general during the Revolutionary War. When 22 years old, in 1754, he was appointed a militia captain, then a justice of the peace, and was a member of the General Assembly in 1760. His training of the militia in Brunswick broke his already strained relations with the new governor, Josiah Martin. The governor denounced Howe, John Ashe, and Harnett for "their unremitted labours to promote sedition and rebellion here from the beginning of the discontents in America, to this time, that they stand foremost among the patrons of revolt and anarchy".

A member of "The Family" and possessing a rice plantation, Howe required help from relatives to stay solvent. He was known to have quite an interest in the ladies and was separated from his wife in an age when this was not accepted. He was considered to be gallant in manners and socially adept.

His interest in the militia led him to introduce legislation to increase funds for its support. Throughout the years before the war he was an important supporter of better military conditions. His legislative skills were highly effective in the judicial changes he introduced for superior courts, in rules for river pilots, and other such diverse subjects as boundary disputes, laws concerning free negroes, pardons for

Cornelius Harnett was a vocal patriot leader who also participated in the attack on Fort Johnston.

Regulators, and deer hunting.

A good friend of the previous governor, Howe had supported legislation to help Tryon keep harmony in the colony. Tryon disliked unpleasantness, so he appreciated Howe's efforts. He gave Howe the command of Fort Johnston and appointed him head of the Court of Exchequer in Wilmington. Howe went to Hillsborough as Quartermaster General with Tryon's army to fight the Regulators.

When Martin replaced Tryon as governor, Howe lost his two local positions. Though he had not been noticeable during the Stamp Act rebellion, at this time he became an active member of the Sons of Liberty. Josiah Quincy referred to him as "hot and zealous in the cause of America".

The people of Brunswick collected food for the citizens of Boston after the British closed that Massachusetts port in the wake of their famous Tea Party in 1774. Richard Quince's son, Parker, offered his ship *Penelope*, free of charge. It was loaded with 2,096 bushels of corn, 22 barrels of flour and 17 barrels of pork and other foodstuffs. Parker Quince captained the

ship himself and sailed for Marblehead, where he delivered the very welcome cargo.

In the winter of 1775 another of Quince's ships, the *Rebecca*, sailed into Brunswick from Scotland and the British West Indies with a passenger who kept a journal that has given us some interesting information about the nine months she remained in the Cape Fear region. This lady was Miss Janet Schaw who was on her way to Wilmington to visit her brother, Robert Schaw. She was welcomed at Richard Quince's home on an unpleasantly cold night. She wrote in her journal, "We got safe ashore, and tho quite dark landed from a boat with little trouble, and proceeded thro'rows of tar and pitch to the house of a mercht, to whom we had been recommended. He received us in a hall which tho not very orderly, had a cheerful look, to which a large carron stove filled with Scotch coals not a little contributed. The night was bitterly cold, and we gathered around the hearth with great satisfaction, and the Master of the house gave us a hospitable welcome. This place is called Brunswick, and tho the best sea port in the province, the town is very poor – a few scattered houses on the edge of the woods, without street or regularity. These are inhabited by merchants, of whom Mr. Quense our host is the first in consequence. He is deeply engaged in the newe system of politicks, in which they all are more or less, tho Mr. Dry, the collector of the customs, is the most zealous, and talks treason by the hour."

While Miss Schaw was in the area she met Robert Howe and noted in her hournal that he could easily be a leader of the army and added that such an army was indeed being formed. She watched some of the "bush training" but was not impressed with the lack of uniforms or the methods of training.

In June 1775, Governonr Josiah Martin fled from New Bern in fear of his life when demonstrations against British rule erupted. He went to Fort Johnston for safety but, due to the lack of any noticeable support from the Loyalists, he decided to take refuge on board His Majesty's ship *Cruizer*, anchored in the river on July 19, 1775. Two months later, armed men led by Cornelius Harnett, John Ashe, and Robert Howe attacked and burned the fort. Some of the fleet sailed for Charleston, South Carolina and took Martin with them. This was the end of British rule in North Carolina.

After the royal government failed, a Provincial Congress ruled in North Carolina. There was very little change in the membership or in the way legislative business was handled. A Committee of Safety was appointed to be in charge of each town and county. Richard Quince was the chairman in Brunswick and was in office by June of 1775.

Royal Governor Josiah Martin

Also, a Committee of Correspondence was established for the purpose of keeping all the colonies aware of happenings and giving them moral support in the struggle for their beliefs. Each county was asked to elect men to go as representatives to meetings for deciding policies and actions. Robert Howe and James Moore were on this committee.

The Provincial Congress had voted to boycott goods from England after North Carolina had been exempted from Parliament's Restraining Acts which prohibited trade with the West Indies and England in early 1775. This pointed out the continued need of naval stores by England's great navy.

Colonial Records contain a message sent from the Continental Congress showing concern that some people might be tempted to capitalize on this exemption. "Do you ask why then you are exempted from the Penalties of the Bill restraining Trade? The Reason is obvious – Britain cannot keep up its Naval Force without you; you supply the very sinews of her strength. Restrain your Naval Stores and all the Powers of Europe can scarcely supply her; restrain them and you strengthen the hands of America in the glorious contention for her Liberty. Through you the Minister wishes to disunite the whole Colonial Link; we know your virtue too well to dread his success."

Due to the unstable conditions, as early as September 1774 delegates from most colonies had met in Philadelphia. A Continental Association was formed and the members agreed that all imports from Britain should be stopped by the end of that year. Also agreed was that exports would be halted a few months later. Those colonists who broke this boycott would find their names on public papers for all to see and censure.

Of local interest, the Committee of Safety asked each merchant to refrain from selling boycotted items. It was understood by all citizens that sacrifices were to be made for the success of their cause. Of course, the Loyalists were against this. There was a merchant named Dunbibbin who had sold salt. Evidently he saw the error of his ways since a record survives telling of his offer to return the money he had made. This indicates public sentiment and the power of the local patriots.

Though the Revolutionary Was began on April 18, 1775, it was May 8 when Cornelius Harnett received papers from Massachusetts that had been sent by riders through each colonial town. He sent them from Wilmington to Richard Quince in Brunswick, requesting him to send them south by the quickest method. Quince sent the papers that same night to the South Carolina towns.

Brunswick, May 8, 1775
9 o'clock in the evening

To Mr. Isaac Marion:

Sir:

I take the liberty to forward by express the enclosed papers which I just received from Wilmington and I must entreat you to forward them to your committee at Georgetown to be conveyed to Charleston from yours with speed. Enclosed is the newspaper giving account of the beginning of the battle (of Lexington) and a letter of what happened after. Pray don't neglect a moment in forwarding it.

I am your humble servant,

Richard Quince

Soon after this a message was reported to have been intercepted saying that a large group of Tories were to gather at Fort Johnston. Even after the commander of the fort moved or destroyed the cannon there, almost 500 patriots under the leadership of Robert Howe left Brunswick for the fort and burned it. The irony was that the fort could have been used later to keep the British out of the river.

Local people were very uneasy with British ships on the river. Rumors abounded and fears of attack became very real. Brunswick inhabitants began packing up their belongings and moving to safer areas such as Wilmington.

There is a 1775 letter from this time from Mrs. DeRosset of Wilmington, to John Burgwin that states, "Mr. Lord of Brunswick talks of taking (a house in Wilmington). Indeed most of the Brunswick people, they say, talk of coming up here soon".

In the Colonial Records of 1775 it was noted that British men-of-war were at Fort Johnston and their leaders intended to burn Brunswick and advance upon Wilmington.

Also, there is an affidavit written in February 1776 by William Rawdon that as he stood aboard one of these warships, he was told by two officers that "they had intended that night to go up to the town of Brunswick, with about 100 sailors, to set the town on fire in front, station their men on the back of the town, and destroy man, woman and child, that escaped from the flames; but the reason they did not put their design in execution was that a British vessel went aground, and by the time it was freed (the British officer learned) that the inhabitants had left the town, and therefore it was no use to burn it." This unhappy account was published in the *Virginia Gazette* on March 22, 1776. From the same newspaper the following article appeared on April 5, 1776.

"Captain Collett (British) has lately committed diverse acts of piracy and robbery. Amongst others he set fire to the elegant house of Col. Dry...destroying therein all the valuable furniture, liquors, etc..."

And on the same date this article appeared.

"The Town of Brunswick is totally deserted, and the enemy frequently land in small parties, to pillage and carry off Negroes..."

Some forays were made by the British soldiers into the town to look for anything of value. A large group led by Generals Clinton and Cornwallis marched on Robert Howe's plantation, Kendall, where it was reported they mistreated the women. Howe and James Moore had become important officers in the North Carolina militia and when that became part of the

Continental command both were promoted to brigadier general. Thus Howe's home was a natural target for the British forces.

Brunswick was destroyed and Lockwood's Folly became the county seat for a few years.

In March and April of 1776, British forces gathered for an attack but Clinton and Cornwallis realized the Tories could not defeat the Patriots after losing a decisive battle at Moores Creek Bridge a few miles away. They did not have the manpower.

Before leaving the region Gen. Clinton thought to gain some support by granting a pardon to any Patriot who would lay down his guns. It is interesting to note that the only exclusions to this offer were Cornelius Harnett and Robert Howe, two sons of Brunswick.

As can be realized, for several years Brunswick had dealt with uncertainty and restlessness. A number of men with property in or near the town had led the way toward independence. Some were influential and powerful enough to make an enormous difference in the future of the nation.

From the Stamp Act rebellion onward the lines were drawn between colonists who were loyal to England and those who wanted independence. Those who continued to support the King during the war had their property confiscated by the new government after the Revolution.

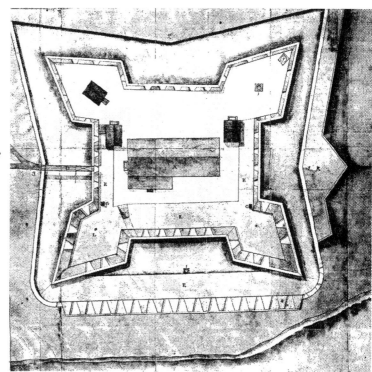

The plans of Fort Johnston as it appeared during the Revolutionary War. Men from Brunswick and Wilmington destroyed the fort to keep it from the British.

The Federal attack on Fort Anderson in February 1865, just weeks after the fall of Fort Fisher, left the installation built on the ruins of Brunswick as the only obstacle between Yankee troops and Wilmington.

Fort Anderson

Johnson Hagood watched through his field glasses as the tiny blue dots swarmed over what had been the Confederacy's most formidable fort. Up until a week ago, the South Carolina general had been on leave. But when Union troops under General Alfred Terry succeeded in capturing Fort Fisher, Hagood had been hastily recalled. Louis Hebert, the Confederate brigadier from Louisiana, had been relieved of command at Fort Anderson, just north of Fort Fisher on the west bank of the Cape Fear River, after concerns about his actions and reports of drunkenness. Now Hagood had the responsibility of blunting the Yankee strike that was aimed at the South's last open port at Wilmington.

Fort Anderson began life on the site of the Cape Fear's early settlement at Brunswick. The colonial town had thrived as the official port of entry to the colony until being overshadowed by Wilmington, fourteen miles upriver. By 1776, when British troops raided the town and destroyed much of what was there, all but a few families had relocated to other parts. In 1862, Confederate Brigadier General Samuel Gibbs French ordered Major Thomas Rowland to begin construction of what would become the second largest of the several forts and gun batteries built to safeguard access to the port at Wilmington.

Rowland was something of a gifted engineer, ranked high among his West Point classmates before resigning his commission in the U.S. Army and accepting a new one in the army of the rebelling Confederate States. He took to the project with zeal, and soon had the beginnings of a formidable

Col. William Lamb

fortress rising above the ruins where royal governors had once lived. Among the junior officers assigned to help in the task was a young and energetic Virginian from Norfolk, William Lamb. He would command Fort Anderson for a brief time after Major Rowland was transferred out of the Cape Fear District, before himself being assigned to take over what would become the centerpiece of the river defenses, Fort Fisher. The two officers shared an affinity for military engineering. Much of what Lamb later incorporated into the construction of Fort Fisher undoubtedly came from lessons learned from Rowland during the construction of what initially was named Fort St. Philip (for the remains of the colonial church on the site).

It was a good site for a fort. High on a bluff overlooking the mile-wide river, Confederates could effectively shut down the waterway with heavy guns and torpedoes. Orton Pond, at the rear of the fort, created an obstacle to flanking attacks that would make a land assault difficult. Coupled with other strategically placed gun batteries on both banks of the river, the Confederates created a gauntlet of hot lead that would shred any Union warships trying to ascend up to Wilmington.

When William H.C. Whiting succeeded French as commander of the Cape Fear District, he set about improving on the good start already underway to fortify the river. He also ordered that all fortifications in the district be given names that commemorated the "...many distinguished and gallant dead of North Carolina." With the order, Fort St. Philip was re-christened Fort Anderson. Up until the late 20th century, historians believed the fort to have been named in honor of BrigGen Joseph Reid Anderson, owner of the Tredegar Iron Works in Richmond and for a time the commander of the Cape Fear District. Recent evidence makes that assumption unlikely, however. At the time Whiting ordered the fort renamed, Joseph R. Anderson was still very much alive, so it is unlikely that he met the criteria set by Whiting of being among the "gallant dead." Current thought is that the fort was named after BrigGen George Burgwyn Anderson, who fell at the Battle of Sharpsburg in 1862. George B. Anderson was a direct descendant of John Burgwyn, the colonial merchant whose house is said to have served as headquarters for British General Sir Charles Cornwallis during the occupation of Wilmington in the Revolutionary War.

Fort Anderson was an impressive obstacle for Union war planners tasked with taking Wilmington. For three years prior to the fall of Fort Fisher, rebel troops, with conscripted and leased slave labor from surrounding plantations, built the imposing traverses that would house the fort's main batteries. Orton Plantation's owner, Thomas C. Miller, Jr., played host to Rowland and his officers while the fort was under construction. Rowland's design called for two main batteries of five heavy 32lb seacoast guns each. Battery A ran parallel to the Cape Fear River, while Battery B ran at an angle from the riverfront through the ruins of Brunswick, over 800 yards to Orton Pond. The guns of the two batteries could repel attacks from the river or on land from the south, while smaller mobile artillery pieces covered the line of works stretching to Orton Pond and to the rear. These smaller guns included 12lb Napoleon field pieces. A 12lb Whitworth mounted on a mobile field carriage was a particularly formidable weapon,

capable of launching a rifled shell 3000 yards with deadly accuracy. The British designed Whitworth cannon had earned a healthy respect from Union naval officers who found themselves on the receiving end of their fire during the blockade off Fort Fisher. Rifle pits, abatis and other light artillery pieces completed the defenses of Fort Anderson.

Swampy land that included several ponds and bogs, populated by a large number of alligators and poisonous snakes, were Mother Nature's contribution to Fort Anderson's defenses. Orton Pond was actually more like a lake, an imposing obstacle that would force

BrigGen George Burgwyn Anderson

MajGen WHC Whiting

an attacker to travel more than twelve miles around, through truly wicked thickets, brambles and swamps, in order to execute a flank attack on the fort. This fact left Confederate engineers confident that their rear would be secure – an assumption that would cost them dearly when Union troops began their march to Wilmington.

Rowland and Lamb built barracks for the Fort Anderson garrison, using ballast stones from the 18th Century sailing ships that had called on Brunswick, for chimneys. Soldiers pried loose other stones from the ruins of Brunswick houses and incorporated them into the fort construction. The buildings themselves were wood, and to date more than fifty chimney ruins have been found at the fort site.

Prior to the first Union attempt to reduce the Cape Fear defenses, on Christmas Eve 1864, the Yankee blockade lurked offshore like a dark menace always just out of reach. Occasionally that menace would attempt through guile what they were not able to accomplish by main force of arms. Union raiding and reconnaissance parties would sometimes slip into the Cape Fear River using small boats and moonless nights to tweak the noses of the Confederates manning Forts Fisher and Anderson. One of the most daring of these northern interlopers was Lieutenant Commander William B. Cushing, a rising star in the U.S. Navy widely known for his successful destruction of the Confederate ram *C.S.S. Albemarle* on the Neuse River earlier in the war. Dubbed "Lincoln's Commando" by admirers, Cushing would play a central role in the Wilmington Campaign that saw the fall of Fort Anderson.

After the fall of Fort Fisher, Union forces were able to consolidate their hold on the east bank of the river, while Northern warships and gunboats were able to enter the Cape Fear itself for the first time. Once that side of the river was secure, their attention turned to Fort Anderson. On February 17, 1865 the U.S. Navy began a bombardment of the fort that lasted all day. When it ended, the battered defenders celebrated with a concert for Colonel John Hedrick, the much-liked commander of the 40th North Carolina troops who made up the bulk of the Anderson garrison. When the concert ended, Hedrick asked a Col. Taylor to extend his thanks to the musicians of the Eutaw Band attached to the 25th South Carolina. As Taylor gave his brief speech to thank the men and offer encouragement for the fight they all knew was coming, no one noticed a dark-clad figure hunched below one of the big seacoast guns a scant seventy-five feet from the assembled Confederates. William B. Cushing listened attentively while Taylor gave his speech. He noted the disposition of the fort's troops and cannon, and then quietly slipped back to his boat waiting in a cove just north of the fort. Cushing and his crew rowed back downriver after again being spotted and fired on by Fort Anderson's sentries. But the Reb troops never knew how close the daring Yankee naval officer had been until weeks later, when a captured northern newspaper recounted the visit.

Col. John Hedrick

John Hedrick had assumed command of Fort Anderson after Rowland and Lamb were transferred out. A former shopkeeper from Wilmington, Hedrick was much loved by his men and an ardent secessionist. He led Cape Fear rebel militia in the seizing of Forts Johnston and Caswell weeks before the firing on Fort Sumter. Hedrick realized that war between the North and South was coming, and wanted to eliminate any federal installations in North Carolina's own backyard before they could be used to launch attacks against the rebels. Because the state technically wasn't at war yet, North Carolina's governor made Hedrick give the forts back to their Yankee caretakers. Weeks later, after the fall of Fort Sumter, President Abraham

Lincoln called on North Carolina to provide men to suppress the rebellion. When that order came, North Carolina joined her sister states in secession, and Hedrick was ordered to reoccupy the forts at the mouth of the Cape Fear. As commander of Fort Anderson, Hedrick labored long and hard to enhance the fort's ability to control the Cape Fear River, enlarging earthworks and land defenses, and fortifying the river itself with floating mines called torpedoes, and other obstructions to navigation designed to thwart any river-borne push on Wilmington.

As the war went on, both sides were increasingly aware of the importance of the port at Wilmington. The Union blockade had slowly choked off the other ports at Savannah, Charleston and Mobile. Robert E. Lee made it plain that his army depended entirely on the goods and munitions brought in through Wilmington to remain in the field. For the South, Wilmington must be held. For the North, the fall of Wilmington would make a Confederate surrender just a matter of time. Secretary of the Navy Gideon Welles had long wanted to mount an expedition against Fort Fisher and Wilmington, but General Ulysses S. Grant had more pressing needs for the land forces that would be required for the attack to succeed. But by the fall of 1864, Grant was ready to turn his attention to the Cape Fear. An expedition led by Admiral David Dixon Porter and Major General Benjamin Butler assembled at Hampton Roads, Virginia and set sail to take on the mighty Fort Fisher in December. The expedition seemed doomed from the beginning.

Butler and Porter did not get along, and the two men seemed to go out of their way to stick it to each other. Butler had devised a scheme to use a ship laden with gunpowder to blow a hole in Fort Fisher, which Admiral Porter detonated himself before Butler could arrive off the Cape Fear coast. The explosion did little more than disturb the sleep of Col. Lamb's garrison and provide Fort Fisher's defenders with a good laugh. The next day, Union troops began landing north of the fort while U.S. warships began trading shots with the Confederates. After a day of shelling, Butler decided the fort could not be taken by a land assault and ordered his men back to their transports. The Union fleet turned back for Hampton Roads, while rebel defenders stood atop Fort Fisher's traverses and played "Dixie" as a parting salute.

The embarrassment of the Christmas Eve expedition finally served to cement Grant's determination to take Fort Fisher. Two weeks later, in January 1865, the Union fleet was back. This time the army contingent was under the capable command of Brevet Brigadier General Alfred Terry. Porter and Terry got along famously, unlike his predecessor, the political general Butler. After delivering what up until that time was the heaviest naval bombardment in history, Terry landed his men and took Fort Fisher by storm after a daylong fight. When Major James Reilly tendered his sword in surrender at Battery Buchanan, on behalf of the wounded William Lamb and Gen. W.H.C. Whiting, everyone knew Fort Anderson would be next in the Union crosshairs.

The Yankees spent much of the next month consolidating their gains. Confederate troops at Forts Holmes, Pender, Caswell and Campbell all were withdrawn to join the garrison at Fort Anderson. With Fort Fisher gone and the Yankees in control of New Inlet, the enemy was in their rear, and that made the lower river forts untenable. Union gunboats began appearing regularly, slipping forward to lob a shell or two at Fort Anderson, testing the river defenses while Northern generals decided how best to crack the next link in the Cape Fear defense chain.

LtCmdr William B. Cushing
from the collection of Dr. Chris E. Fonvielle, Jr.

LtCmdr Cushing took possession of the deserted Oak Island forts on January 18, 1865. By the next day, Union forces were in control of everything from Old Inlet up to Battery Lamb, a scant four miles below Fort Anderson. With the enemy so close, General Hebert asked Cape Fear District commander Braxton Bragg for a cavalry picket to screen Ft. Anderson's western flank. Bragg, busy evacuating Wilmington after failing to save Fort Fisher, sent a small number of horsemen from the 2nd South Carolina Cavalry. The Confederate defenders at the fort were ordered by Bragg to "...not give up your present position" unless it became necessary to do so to save the men from capture.

By February 1865, roughly 2,300 men defended Fort Anderson. Most were part of the 40th North Carolina State Troops, along with stragglers gathered from the retreating garrisons of the installations at the mouth of the river. Among these were 900 men from Fort Caswell, plus elements of the 2nd South Carolina Cavalry, Mosely's Battery and Bradham's Light Battery. As the blue tide gathered to the south, men from both sides cursed the

Johnson Hagood

dismal January and early February weather often experienced along the Cape Fear coast. Cold rain and chilly temperatures spread their discomfort equally between Johnny Rebs and Billy Yanks alike. The bad weather hampered the landing of Gen. John Schofield's XXIII Corp divisions, sent by Ulysses S. Grant to reinforce the army already on the Cape Fear in the coming advance. But by mid-month, Terry's anxious Union forces, under the overall command of newly appointed John Schofield, were ready to begin the march to Wilmington.

The Yankee plan called for a two-pronged pincher attack that would move up the river from both the east and west sides to attack Wilmington. While Union forces that included Charles Paine's U.S. Colored Troops advanced up the newly renamed Federal Point peninsula on the east, other elements under General Jacob Cox and John Schofield would march up the Brunswick County side, reducing Fort Anderson and converging on the target city across Eagle Island.

To do it, they sent more than 6,000 men up the road to the Brunswick ruins. Hagood's South Carolina cavalry began skirmishing with the advancing Yankees, setting the woods on fire and chopping down trees to slow their advance, while riders delivered word that the enemy was on the move. In the river, the ironclad monitor *U.S.S. Montauk* brazenly sailed abreast of Fort Anderson and calmly weathered a barrage of forty-seven rounds from Hagood's big guns before retiring back downstream. Two months after the fall of Fort Anderson, the *Montauk* would gain notoriety as the place where Abraham Lincoln's body was autopsied after being assassinated by John Wilkes Booth. Booth's co-conspirators would be imprisoned aboard the ironclad pending trial when they were captured. Union gunboats returned to shell the fort and add their signatures to the already bullet-pocked walls of old St. Philips Church. Schofield and Cox used part of their force to fix the Confederate's attention to the front, while another force was sent to skirt Orton Pond and engage the Fort Anderson defenders from the rear.

On the east, Porter's flotilla of shallow draft gunboats and monitors were arrayed off Fort Anderson and began delivering a steady bombardment. Hagood's gunners replied with fire of their own, but were short on ammunition for their best gun, the Whitworth cannon. The inventive William B. Cushing built a phony ironclad over the frame of a wooden hull hoping to lull the rebel defenders into detonating the potentially deadly floating minefield in the river channel, permitting the Union flotilla to advance closer to the fort and Wilmington. The ruse did not fool the Confederates, much to Cushing's disappointment. While shells rained down

The innovative Cushing built a fake monitor to trick Confederate defenders at Fort Anderson into detonating the network of torpedos guarding the river approaches.

on Hagood and his men, U.S. Army troops of Cox's command completed their circumvention of the water obstacle in the fort's rear and gathered for the assault. Another division under the command of General Adelbert Ames joined them, seasoned soldiers who had taken part in the capture of Fort Fisher. The only force they faced was the harassment of the South Carolina cavalry screeners. By February 18, Yankee soldiers were within 600 yards of the fort.

Messages delivered to Hagood from the west told him that a strong Yankee force was about to invest Fort Anderson from the rear, while a frontal assault was forming up from the south. If Cox's troops were allowed

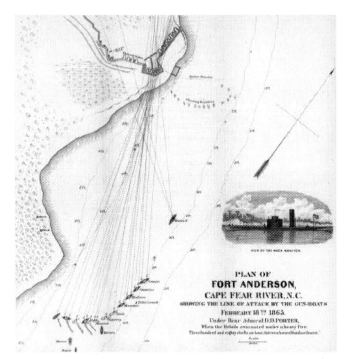

This map shows the disposition of Union gunboats and monitors in the attack on Fort Anderson.

to close off the road to Wilmington, there was nothing to stop them from capturing the Fort Anderson garrison intact or bypassing it completely and marching unopposed to Wilmington.

General Robert F. Hoke, the North Carolina-born officer that Robert E. Lee considered to be one of his best warriors, had assumed command of the Cape Fear District when Braxton Bragg suddenly declared he had business in Richmond. Hagood sent Hoke a message informing him of the situation in Brunswick County and asking for new orders. Hoke looked at a map and instructed Hagood to withdraw his men to a line on the northern bank of Town Creek, seven miles up from the fort, and make a stand there. The Confederates were to delay the Yankee advance as long as they could while Hoke completed the evacuation of all government and military supplies and personnel from Wilmington. With Union General William T. Sherman searing a swath through the interior of the Carolinas, and another Union force pressing on the port city from the south, Hoke knew Wilmington was lost. The best he could do was salvage what he could in the face of a bad tactical situation and overwhelming odds.

Quietly on the night of February 18, Johnson Hagood began slipping his 2,200 men out of the fort and up the road to Town Creek. It was a hasty withdrawal that didn't even leave time for the harried southerners to spike their cannons. The last Confederates slipped out of the post around dawn,

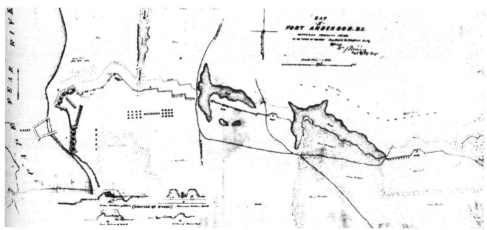

The Confederate earthworks of Fort Anderson stretched for miles, including Orton Pond as an obstacle to attack.

leaving only about fifty men as a rearguard to face the oncoming federal assault. When it became light enough, a blue tide swept toward the Fort Anderson traverses, rolling unopposed over the mounds of Battery B. Naval gunfire began to split the air as Porter's gunboats lent their support to the attack, not realizing that federals had already taken their objective. As shells began bursting over their heads, Union soldiers frantically ran to the tops of the traverses, waiving white flags to signal the flotilla to cease fire. Fort Anderson had fallen, but in doing so became the only Confederate fort to be surrendered by the U.S. Army to the U.S. Navy.

On the west, it was hours later that General Cox learned the fort had been abandoned and was now in Union hands. He aimed his forces at Town Creek and the two sides engaged in a brief but ferocious fight before Hagood's Confederates retreated again to Wilmington. Three days later, Union soldiers crossed the Cape Fear River and landed at the foot of Market Street to at last occupy Wilmington.

Battery B as it appears today. Fort Anderson is considered one of the best preserved Confederate forts left today.

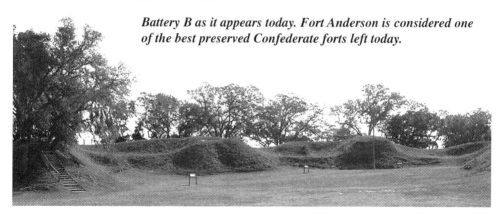

The original Fort Anderson flag, which flew over the fort in its final battle in 1865.

The Fort Anderson Flag

While Union shells scorched the air above Fort Anderson and Confederate cannons hurled their own deadly replies, the broad white field of the garrison flag flapped defiantly from the parade ground flagpole, easily visible over the tops of the traverses. In the top inner corner, the red, white and blue of the Stars and Bars battle flag represented the 2nd National Flag of the Confederate States of America, more commonly referred to as "the Stainless Banner". The flag earned that name from the romantic notion that no dishonor could possibly attach itself to the flag and the cause it represented. Johnson Hagood and his outnumbered and undersupplied men did their best to uphold its honor at Fort Anderson, until a Union flanking movement around Orton Pond made the situation at the fort untenable. As the Confederates hastily evacuated the fort on the night of February 18, 1865, someone hurriedly lowered the flag and thrust it into a wagon headed for Wilmington.

When the sun came up the next day, Union forces were surprised to find Fort Anderson empty. They resumed their march up the west side of the Cape Fear River, fighting at Town Creek for two days on the way. On the march north, a soldier of Company A, 140th Indiana Infantry, spotted what looked like a crumpled sheet lying on the road to Wilmington. He picked it up and discovered it was the same garrison flag that had flown over Fort Anderson the day before. The tired soldier recognized a neat souvenir when he saw one, and quickly shoved it into his pack. That night he turned the flag over to his commanding officer, Colonel Thomas J. Brady.

A month later, after the fall of Wilmington, Brady presented the trophy flag to Indiana's governor, Oliver P. Morton, at a ceremony in Washington, D.C. President Abraham Lincoln attended the event to show his gratitude for Morton's steady support during the war. Lincoln's visit prompted the cancellation of a previously scheduled visit to a play staged at

John Wilkes Booth

Campbell Hospital near the Washington Soldier's Home. Unknown to Lincoln and his staff, a disaffected Southern sympathizer and actor named John Wilkes Booth had planned to kidnap the President during that visit. When Lincoln chose to attend the review of the 140th Indiana instead, Booth decided to change his plans to a more deadly scheme. Not long afterward, the deranged Booth shot and killed Abraham Lincoln during a performance of "My American Cousin" at Ford's Theater in the nation's capitol.

For more than a century ownership of the Fort Anderson flag changed, until in 2004 it was offered for sale by an antiquities dealer in Pennsylvania. Authenticated by flag and textile experts, the dealer put an asking price of $40,000 on the Fort Anderson flag. Several museums showed an interest in the flag, as did the Brunswick Town / Fort Anderson State Historic Site. With North Carolina state coffers bare due to tight budgets, historic site personnel began a fundraising drive to buy the flag and bring it home. Within months Site Director James Bartley and his staff had secured pledges and donations equal to half the asking price. The rest of the money soon followed, and the Fort Anderson Garrison flag assumed its place of honor in the visitors center at Brunswick Town / Fort Anderson State Historic Site, one hundred and forty years after a tired and dirty soldier found it on the road to Wilmington.

President Abraham Lincoln may have signed his death warrant when he chose to attend the Fort Anderson flag presentation instead of making his scheduled visit to comfort wounded soldiers.

The exhibit hall at Brunswick Town / Fort Anderson tells a story that stretches for more than two centuries.

Present Day

Perhaps the most striking quality of colonial Brunswick Town has been its ability to survive amidst devastation and disaster. As a living town, Brunswick withstood Spanish marauders and British burning. After the Revolution, the building fell into ruin, but a special providence seemed to guard what remained. Confederate soldiers erected Fort Anderson across the town site in 1862. Trees and underbrush protected the remains of Brunswick from the elements until a new threat emerged in the late 1940s from the United States government. The Sunny Point Army Terminal was to be built on land adjoining a buffer area. The town site at that time belonged to J. Laurence Sprunt, owner of Orton Plantation. The Sprunt family had for years possessed a keen interest in the history of the Cape Fear area. Sprunt undoubtedly was influenced also by the active work of Dr. E. Lawrence Lee, who began a crusade to preserve remains to merit preservation; Sprunt then donated 114 1/2 acres for the 119-acre tract to the state for a historic site. The Episcopal Diocese of East Carolina gave the remaining 5 acres at Brunswick Town, including St. Philips Church, to the state.

Plans for development of Brunswick Town were being formulated by Archives and History when complications arose. The military installation at

Sunny Point objected to a full restoration project at their back door, so to speak, and the result was a restrictive easement between North Carolina and the United States. This 1957 agreement provides for a buffer zone within the historic district over which the federal government exercises restrictive control. No new structures may be erected, nor changes made in the landscape, without permission of the commanding officer at Sunny Point. The safety zone lies in the heart of the historic site and over the years has affected development plans.

In June 1958 Archives and History employed Dr. Lee to make a site survey in preparation for extensive archeological excavation. He cleared much of the growth from the area and mapped most of the existing ruins as well as the earthen walls of Fort Anderson. Excavation began late that summer under Stanley South, staff archaeologist. South plotted the entire archaeological project and for more than ten years worked to carry it toward completion. State officials agreed that Brunswick Town should remain an archaeological interpretation. Over the years twenty-three of sixty foundations were excavated and preserved for the viewing public.

The state appropriated $10,000 in 1961, and the Smith Richardson Foundation gave a supporting grant of $5,000 to begin clearing the earthen walls of Fort Anderson.

In 1965 the General Assembly appropriated funds for a site manager's residence. No satisfactory location could be agreed upon with either Sunny Point or the Sprunt heirs, and Archives and History was forced to abandon the plan. Instead a chain link fence was constructed around the site in 1966 to protect it from vandalism and theft.

It was not until 1963 that the legislature appropriated $80,000 for a visitor center. The commander at Sunny Point granted permission for the facility (which stands in the safety zone), and the center was formally dedicated on April 23, 1967. The initial development of Brunswick Town State Historic Site was completed.

In the mid-1970s stabilization of the ruins of St. Philips Church, the most substantial surviving structure at the site, was finished. A federal grant furnished funds for the stabilization of earthen Fort Anderson, fencing of all archaeological ruins, and clearing of several acres between the fort and the Cape Fear River.

During the early 1980s the staff expanded relations with local schools and instituted living history demonstrations at Heritage Days as well as teacher workshops.

Brunswick Town consists of the ruins of St. Philips Church, twenty-three excavated foundations of the colonial town out of a total of sixty, a visitor center, Civil War earthworks of Fort Anderson, and a trail. The foundations have been excavated, and artifacts are on exhibit in the visitor center. The foundations excavated by Stanley South can be seen along the walking tour. The story of the rise and fall of the town, as well as the fort, is told in the visitor center through exhibits and an audiovisual program. In 1996, wayside exhibits were completed, as well as an outdoor visitor station for use by students, special groups, and the public. This shelter is constructed in close concordance with the early 18th century homes.

The site has several programs during the year which highlight different aspects of the colonial period and the Civil War. In 2000, a major renovation of the Visitor's Center was completed. In 2004, new exhibits were installed there, replacing the original "temporary" exhibits.

Conclusion

*B*runswick left quite a legacy for its brief existence. Being one of only a few towns in North Carolina during the early colonial days, it brought much trade and wealth to the state. Its founders helped form and put into practice ideas concerning individual rights under a constitution.

There were obstacles that kept the town from living up to its original projections and the dreams of its founders. However, it was a major seaport; important events took place there; and initiatives were taken toward United States independence from Great Britain that spread to all parts of the thirteen colonies.

Influential men came from Brunswick who proved to be distinguished in government and in war: Major General Robert Howe, Cornelius Harnett II, General James Moore, Judge Maurice Moore, U.S. Supreme Court Justice Alfred Moore, William Dry, and Richard Quince.

Such men as these gave Brunswick an importance far greater than its size and current condition might suggest.

A Brunswick Timeline

1663	King Charles II made large land grants to eight wealthy supporters, the Lords Proprietors
1665	Early settlers from Barbados
1712	Distinction first made between North and South Carolina
1714-1727	King George I of England, alsso Duke of Brunswick in Germany
1718	Stede Bonnet, pirate, captured on the Cape Fear River
1724-1725	George Burrington appointed governor by proprietors; cleared the way for settlers
1725	Maurice Moore received land grants; laid out plot plan for town of Brunswick
1726	Cornelius Harnett bought first lots in town
1727-1760	King George II
1729	New Hanover County established
	Lords Proprietors surrendered charter to King
1731-1734	Burrington appointed first royal governor
1731	Port of Brunswick and town officially recognized
1732	George Washington born
1734-1752	Gabriel Johnston was royal governor of North Carolina
1735	Final boundary settled between North and South Carolina
1741	St. Philips Parish created
1740	County seat moved from Brunswick to Wilmington
1745	Town of Brunswick incorporated
1748	Spanish attack Brunswick
1754	St. Philips Church construction began
1758	Governor Arthur Dobbs moved to Brunswick
1760	George III became King of England
	Governor Dobbs decreed St. Philips His Majesty's Church in North Carolina
1761,1769	Hurricanes destroy many ships and buildings in town
1764	Brunswick County created
1765-1766	Stamp Act resistance at Brunswick Town
1765	William Tryon became royal governor, lived in Brunswick
1768	St. Philips church completed and dedicated
1769	C. J. Sauthier's map of Brunswick drawn
1770	Governor Tryon moved to New Bern
1775	Royal government over; Gov. Martin flees New Bern, comes to Cape Fear aboard a Royal Navy ship
1776	Brunswick Town deserted, British burn some buildings
1842	Brunswick Town site sold to Frederick Hill for $4.25 by the State of North Carolina to become part of Orton Plantation

1862	Fort Anderson built over town ruins
1865	Attack by Union forces; Fort Anderson evacuated
1880	Episcopal Diocese obtains St. Philips Church ruins
1951	Sprunt Family donated 114 acres of town to the state
	Episcopal Diocese donated church and 5 acres to the state
1955	Brunswick Town State Historic Site established
1958	Archaeological excavation began under Stanley South of the North Carolina Department of Archives and History
1967	Brunswick Town Visitors Center and Museum opened and dedicated
2000	Major renovation of Visitor's Center completed
2004	New exhibits installed, replacing original temporary exhibits

Buried in St. Philips Church Cemetery

Governor Arthur Dobbs, died 1765, unmarked grave within the walls

Mrs. Mary Quince, died 1762, at age 34, wife of Richard

Mrs. Jane Quince, died 1763, at age 19, wife of John

Richard Quince, died 1783

William Dry III, died 1781, at age 61

Mrs. Mary Dry, died 1793, at age 64, wife of William

Mrs. Rebecca McGwire, died 1766, at age 17, daughter of Wm. Dry, wife of Thomas McGwire

Benjamin Smith, died 1826, at age 70, Governor of N.C.

Mrs. Mary Bacot, died 1838, at age 75

John Lord, native of Brunswick, died 1831, at age 66

Mrs. Elizabeth Lord, wife of John, died 1847, at age 84

Alfred Moore, grandson of the founder and native of Brunswick, born 1755, died 1810, at age 55. N.C. Attorney-General, Judge of N.C. Superior Court, U.S. Supreme Court Justice

William Hill, died 1783, at age 47

Mrs. Margaret Hill, died 1788, at age 54, wife of William, also their infant children – Anna, Henry, William, Maurice, and Maurice Moore.

Mrs. Elizabeth Hill, died 1788, at age 26, wife of W.H. Hill

Mrs. Elizabeth Eagan, died 1785, at age 64

Mrs. Elizabeth Guerard, died 1775, at age 18, wife of John

John Guerard, died 1798, at age 45

Mrs. Rebecca Maxwell, died 1810, at age 49, former wife of John Guerard

Peter Maxwell, died 1812, at age 59, native of Scotland

Descriptions of Some Inhabitants

Christopher Cain: 1759 Searcher, 1760 Patroller, Blacksmith 1763, Coroner 1769, Sheriff 1772, Planter 1775. Opposed Revolution. When the new state of North Carolina was established all of his twenty-two hundred acres were confiscated.

William Dry II: moved to Brunswick with his family, including his 15 year old son Wm. III in 1735. His wife was Rebecca Moore, sister of Roger, Nathaniel, and Maurice. Bought several lots and lived there as a merchant. Served as justice of the peace and was captain of militia. Died about 1747.

William Dry III: In 1748 at age 28 was captain of the militia and led the counter-attack against the Spaniards who had surprised and invaded Brunswick. Became a colonel in 1754; was appointed Collector of the Port in 1761. Served in the Assembly 1760-62; became a member of the council from 1764 to 1775 when Gov. Martin suspended him for disloyalty to the crown. When new constitution was adopted he accepted seat on revolutionary council. 1751 appointed to collect and apply subscriptions toward building a church in Brunswick. Had the idea to use ballast stones to build a causeway on the road to Wilmington from Brunswick. Born 1720, died 1781. He and wife are buried at St. Philips. It was at Dry's residence that Josiah Quincy dined in 1773 and Quincy called it "the house of universal hospitality". Dry was considered loyal to the King until the Stamp Act disturbances in 1766, when Gov. Tryon said of him and some others who were employees of the king, "They have been as assiduous in obstructing the reception of stamps as any inhabitants".

James Fergus: purchased lot 351 from Roger Moore in 1737. Doctor. Entitled to bounty of 400 acres by act of congress 1776 for services.

Cornelius Harnett: Victualer, ferry operator. Purchased lots 22 and 23 from M. Moore on June 30, 1726 for 2 pounds each. Came when the council authorized him to keep a ferry from Brunswick to Haulover. Served as sheriff 1739 to 1741. Served as His Majesty's Justice at the court of Common Pleas 1737-1738.

Cornelius Harnett II: Planter, mill owner. An important figure in the fight for independence. Served in the Continental Congress in 1777.

Charles Hepburn: Purchased lot 71 from Maurice Moore with George Reonalds for 10 shillings April 23, 1734. Was appointed Constable for

Brunswick District in 1737, refused to serve and paid his fine of 10 pounds. Land was confiscated after the Revolution.

William Hill: An active patriot of whom Josiah Quincy, in his journal of 1773, said, "though a crown officer, a man replete with sentiments of general liberty, and warmly attached to the cause of American freedom". Buried at St. Philips with wife Margaret Moore Hill, daughter of Nathaniel Moore. A Harvard graduate who came to Brunswick in 1757 and then became a leading merchant. Was lay reader in St. Philips Church when there was no ordained rector in charge of the church.

William Lord: purchased lot 71 from John Wright for 900 pounds in May, 1748. Purchased lot 125 and 126 from James Fergus for 50 pounds in Nov. 1745. Served for 6 days under command of Wm. Dry during the expulsion of the Spanish Sept. 1748. A colonel of the Brunswick Militia.

Robert Howe: Came from a wealthy planter background; brash in younger days; enjoyed the ladies; great socializer. Effective legislator in Provincial Assembly; believed strongly in civilian rule. Moved from militia colonel to major general in the Revolutionary War. Commander of the fortress of West Point. President of the court martial that tried Benedict Arnold. Close friend of George Washington.

John McDowell: Received lot 36B in Sept. 1768. Minister, buried at St. Philips. Property confiscated after the Revolution.

Maurice Moore: Founder of Brunswick. Remaining in N.C. after the Tuscarora War, he married Elizabeth, daughter of Alexander Lillington and the widow of Samuel Swann. He received grants of thousands of acres of land along the Cape Fear River from Governors Burrington and Everard. Strong willed. Stood for the rights of citizens to rule under a constitution.

Maurice Moore, Jr. Judge: Represented Brunswick County in the Provincial Congress of N.C. in 1775. A member of Assembly for years. Bought and sold property in Brunswick, 1759-1774. Judge in court trials against the Regulators in 1768. Credited with writing a political pamphlet showing the Stamp Act was unconstitutional. "Since the Colonials were not a conquered people, they were entitled to be taxed by their own consent". In 1771 as representative from Brunswick, presented a bill to the Assembly for a road to the Cape Fear River from Charlotte, Sherrill's Ford on the Catawba River, and Salisbury. Educated in New England. Died 1777.

Roger Moore: Came to N.C. with brothers Maurice and Nathaniel. Built a large home on the adjoining property to Brunswick and named it Orton. He became politically powerful as a member of "The Family" and was called "King Roger" for his domineering attitude.

Alfred Moore: Grandson of Maurice, Captain during Revolution, United States Supreme Court Associate Justice. Buried at St. Philips in Brunswick.

Edward Moseley: Col. Moseley owned property in Brunswick. Served as Justice at the Court of Common Pleas.

Thomas Mulford: Owner and Master of vessels carrying good to and from Brunswick. Bought an estate in town known as Prospect Hall on lot 337. Ruins located where he was living in 1767. His schooner, the *Brunswick Packet* was used extensively in trade with Philadelphia.

Thomas Payne, or Paines: shipwright,; **Christopher Wooten**: sailmaker; **David Smeeth**: ship carpenter. Residents of Brunswick. The possibility of a shipyard in Brunswick is suggested by the above residents. The Lord Hyde was completed on the river in 1768 and could have been built on the waterfront lot that Smeeth owned in the southern part of town. In 1774, rigging was received for another vessel under construction.

John or J. Porter: Successful merchant of Virginia. Influential. In 1736 Maurice Moore transferred half his interest in Brunswick to Porter as a gift. Both Porter and Moore were dead by 1745, and a dispute over ownership had arisen among heirs. To encourage sale of lots, title was transferred to a commission (Roger Moore, Edward Moseley, William Dry, Richard Quince, and John Wright). Porter was one who received thousands of acres of land before Richard Everard left the office of governor in 1731.

Richard Quince, Sr.: Was one of the leading merchants and traders of the colony, doing business at Brunswick under the firm name of Richard Quince & Sons, later known as Parker Quince & Co., doing a considerable up-river business. He owned several ships. Was a Commissioner of Brunswick, chairman of the Inferior Court of Please and Quarter Sessions of Brunswick Co., a church warden of St. Philips, a judge of the vice-admiralty, a justice of the peace, and with his son, Richard, a member of the general committee of the Sons of Liberty. He was an active participant in the Revolution, died in 1778, and is buried at St. Philips.

George Reonalds: First bought property in Brunswick in 1734 and was a merchant. He loaned a negro slave to assist in the counter-attack against the

Spanish. The negro was accidentally killed, and Reonalds charged William Dry 45 pounds for the loss. A Tory, his property was confiscated after the Revolution.

Edward Scott: Bought a lot from Nathaniel Moore in 1733. Was mariner, ferry keeper, and ran an ordinary.

Benjamin Smith: colonel in Revolutionary War, Governor of North Carolina. Grand Master of Masons. Aide-de-camp to George Washington in 1776, married Sarah Dry, daughter of William. Wounded by his cousin, Maurice Moore, in a duel at the Boundary House marking the line between North and South Carolina. Namesake of Smithville (modern Southport). Buried at St. Philips. A Masonic memorial marker was placed in St. Philips' cemetery in his honor in 1929.

Gov. Benjamin Smith

Known Property Owners in Brunswick

Allen, Eleazar
Allen, Sarah
Anson, Lord George
Bacot, Mary
Bacot, Peter
Belning, Hugh
Bradley, William
Brown, Thomas
Cain, Christopher
Cains, John
Cains, William
Campbell, hugh
Carter, William
Caulkins, Jonathan
Chalkhill, John
Chester, Nathan
Cowen, Duncan
Crawford
Dick, Thoma
Dry, Margaret
Dry, Mary Jane
Dry, Sarah
Dry, William II
Dry, William, Jr.
Dry, William III
Dry, William, sr.
Dunbibbin, Daniel
Dunbibbin, Junius
Dunn, Richard
Eagan, Darby
Egan, Elizabeth
Ellery, Rachael
Espy, James
Fergus, James
Fergus, John
Fowler, Ann
Fowler, Jane
Gibson, Alex
Gibson, William
Grange, John
Guerard, John
Geurard, Elizabeth
Hamson, Joseph
Harnett, Cornelius, Sr.
Harnett, Cornelius

Hellier, Richard
Hepburn, Charles
Hill, Elizabeth
Hill, Frederick J.
Hill, John
Hill, Margaret
Hill, Nathaniel Moore
Hill, Thomas
Hill, Wm. Henry
Hill, William
Holt, Obediah
Hoskins, Henry
Jeanes, William
Jobson, Mich
Jones, Edward
Leach, James
Lord, Elizabeth
Lord, John
Lord, William
Lott
Lovett, Richard
Lyons, James
Mace, Thomas
Marnan, Margaret
Marnan, Thomas
Marsden, Rufus
Marsh, John & Hannah
Mason, Samuel
Maxwell, Peter
Maxwell, Rebecca
McCorkall, Margaret
McDowell, John
McGwire, Rebecca
McIlhenny, James
McIlhenny, Prudence
McKay, Arthur
McKichland, Donald
McNeil, Neil
Moore, Alfred
Moore, Catherine
Moore, George
Moore, Margaret
Moore, Maurice
Moore, Col. Maurice
Moore, Judge Maurice

Moore, Nathaniel
Moore, Roger
Moore, Sarah
Moore, William
Morton, Ann
Moseley, Edward
Moseley, John
Mulford, Thomas
Mullington, Richard
Munro, Revell
Newman, S.P.
Norton, William
Payne, John
Payne, Thomas, Jr.
Payne, Thomas, Sr.
Porter, John
Potter, Robert
Price, Richard
Quince, Anne
Quince, Jane
Quince, Mary
Quince, Richard, Sr.
Quince, Richard, Jr.
Reonalds, George
Rice, John
Richardson, George
Reid
Roland, George
Scott, Edward
Shubrick, Thomas
Smallwood, James
Smeeth, David
Smith, Sarah Moore
Stone, Angelo
Sturger, Jonathan
Swaine, Jonathan
Taylor, N.
Tryon, William
Watts, James
White, James
White, Thomas
Wilson, Richard
Wooten, Christopher
Wooten, Nathaniel
Wright, John

Bibliography

- *A Brief Chronology of the Lower Cape Fear Through the Civil Was Centering on Brunswick Town and Fort Fisher* by Jane Pleasants
- *A New Geography of North Carolina* by Bill Sharpe 1958
- *A Quest for Glory* by Charles Bennett and & Donald Lennon 1991
- *A Biographical History of North Carolina Vol. 2* by Ashe
- *Book of Wilmington* by Andrew J. Howell 1930, 1959
- *Cape Fear Adventure* by Diane Cobb Cashman 1982
- *Chronicles of the Cape Fear River 1660-1916* by James Sprunt 1916
- *Colonial Brunswick* by Stanley South 1960
- *Colonial North Carolina* by Hugh Lefler & Wm. J. Howell 1973
- *Colonial North Carolina in the Eighteenth Century* by Harry Merrens 1964
- *Fort Anderson: Battle For Wilmington* by Chris E. Fonvielle, Jr 1999
- *Harnett, Hooper and Howe* by Watson, Lawson, Lennon
- *Historical Sketches of North Carolina* by John H. Wheeler
- *History of the Brunswick Ferry* by Wilson Angley 1986
- *Journal of a Lady of Quality* by Janet Schaw, edited by Andrews 1939 NewHaven
- *Namesake* by Robert Mason, Moore Co. Historical Association 1989
- *New Hanover County and Wilmington, North Carolina 1723-1938* by William Lord DeRosset 1938
- *North Carolina History of a Southern State* by Hugh Lefler and Albert Newsome 1954
- *Tales and Traditions of the Lower Cape Fear 1661-1896* by James Sprunt 1896
- *The Cape Fear* by Malcolm Ross
- *The Five Royal Governors of North Carolina 1729-1775* by Blackwell Robinson 1963
- *The History of Brunswick County, North Carolina* by Lawrence Lee 1980
- *The Story of Orton Plantation* by James Sprunt 1958
- *War of Secession* by Johnson Hagood 1910
- *Wilmington-New Hanover Safety Committee Minutes 1774-1776* edited by Leora McEachern & Isabel Williams 1974
- *Council Meeting Minutes-Brunswick, July 13, 1744, April 12, 1753*
- *Courthouse records-Brunswick, Nov. 12, 1734, 1736*
- *Executive Council Minutes-Wilmington, June 5, 1740*
- *Higher Court Minutes 1724-1730*
- *Notes on Town of Brunswick* by Lawrence Lee

- *Records of Executive Council Papers* 1766
- *The "State" magazine* by Paul Pleasant May 19, 1956

Telling The Stories That Tell Our Story...

If you love N.C. history, try these other great Dram Tree Books titles:

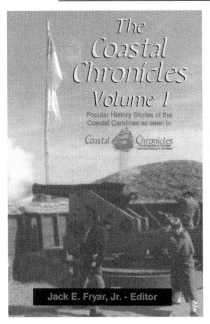

The Coastal Chronicles Volume I

(ISBN 0-9723240-0-3 • $17.95)

All the stories from the first year of *Coastal Chronicles* magazine • Over 80 photos & illustrations, some never before published • Stories by Dr. Chris Fonvielle, Jr., Nicki Leone, Craig Rogers, David Norris, Wendy Smith Bugbee and Jack E. Fryar, Jr. • 27 tales of the Carolina coast including Fort Fisher, the British Occupation of Wilmington, & the Yellow Fever Epidemic of 1862.

"There is great history in these books."

- Hon. Michael F. Easley,
Governor of North Carolina

"...fascinating...an outstanding offering"

- Alan Hodge, Our State Magazine

The Coastal Chronicles Volume II

(ISBN 0-9723240-2-X • $17.95)

The Coastal Chronicles Volume II offers true tales of Blackbeard, the Tuscarora Indian War, plus biographical sketches of home-grown heroes and a lady heroine from the Highlands of Scotland. There are stories here about the British invasion of Beaufort, the African Prince who served a governor, and sleek blockade runners. These stories and more make *The Coastal Chronicles Volume II* a must-have edition!

Get yours at local bookstores or giftshops, or direct from the publisher at:
Dram Tree Books • 2801 Lyndon Ave • Wilmington NC 28405 • dramtreebooks@ec.rr.com

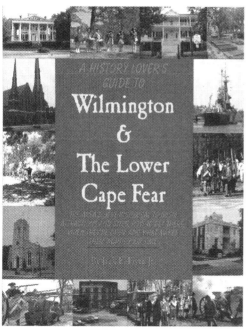

A History Lover's Guide to Wilmington & The Lower Cape Fear
(ISBN 0-9723240-1-1• $17.95)

Over 350 color & historic pictures, many never published before • More than 70 historic sites & attractions in New Hanover, Brunswick, Pender, Columbus & Bladen Counties • Hours of operation, street addresses, maps, contact info & web sites • color coded pages for ease of use • great history in concise write-ups • ferry schedules & yearly special event calendar • Book I of what will be a three-book set covering the entire N.C. coast.

"This is one of the most exciting (and useful) guides to the Cape Fear area to be published in the last ten years...Even long-time residents will find out things they never knew about the people and places in their own backyards."
- Encore Magazine, in selecting **A History Lover's Guide to Wilmington & The Lower Cape Fear** *as one of the best local books of 2003*

Lossing's Pictorial Field-Book of the Revolution in the Carolinas & Georgia
(ISBN 0-9723240-4-6 • $19.95)

The story of the American Revolution in the Carolinas & Georgia told to Lossing by the people who were there. An outstanding chronicle of the skirmishes, battles, heroism, tragedies and atrocities of America's fight for independence. It also provides a rare glimpse into what the country was like in the decade prior to the Civil War. Superbly illustrated with wonderfully informative endnotes.

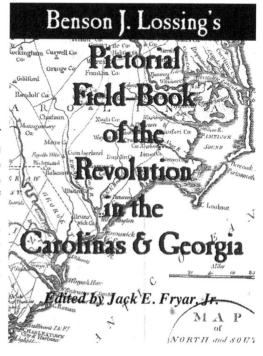

THE indispensable book of Cape Fear history!

Chronicles
of the
Cape Fear River
1660 - 1916

There was a time when the Cape Fear was North Carolina's frontier. The Cape Fear has seen pirates and Indian wars, redcoats and patriot militias, and at least two civil wars. It has sired heroes and villains, statesmen and scholars. Among them was James Sprunt, who as a young man braved the Union blockade as purser aboard a sleek blockade runner. In later life Sprunt became a wealthy businessman whose cotton exporting business was at one time the largest in the world. He owned the storied Orton Plantation, overlooking the river that played such a central role in his life. A philanthropist with a love of the Cape Fear as deep as his very bones, James Sprunt also became widely recognized as one of North Carolina's most respected historians. In what many consider to be the crowning achievement of a distinguished career, *Chronicles of The Cape Fear River: 1667-1916* is the monumental history of southeastern North Carolina that is the starting point for all research into the Cape Fear's varied and colorful past. It is the one book that any true lover of Cape Fear history absolutely must have on their bookshelves, and that all historical researchers should turn to when exploring what came before us, here where the river meets the sea.

CPSIA information can be obtained
at www.ICGtesting.com
Printed in the USA
BVHW040023230419
546193BV00003B/12/P